Original title:
Soil Between My Fingers

Author: Charles Whitfield
ISBN HARDBACK: 978-1-80581-892-2
ISBN PAPERBACK: 978-1-80581-419-1
ISBN EBOOK: 978-1-80581-892-2

Fingers in the Warmth of the Past

Digging in the dirt, what do I find?
Worms authorize a dance, oh so unrefined.
Memories of mud pies when I was a child,
Now my fingers are smeared, looking quite wild.

Seeds of laughter sprout in this place,
Tangled in weeds, I can't keep pace.
My garden's a jungle, no doubt that it's true,
Can I grow a pizza? That might be my cue.

A Symphony of Textures

Fingers feel fingers, what a funny thought,
Rocky, gritty, sticky, I’ve got quite a lot.
Textures collide beneath my touch,
Each one a little from the past, so much!

Peeking through layers, oh vibrant delight,
A mystery unfolds under morning light.
Poking and prodding, what’s hidden down there?
Last year’s lunch? No wonder it’s rare!

Nurturing Nature's Bounty

With a sprinkle of love and a dash of cheer,
I coax out the veggies, "C'mon, don't be shy here!"
Turnips and carrots giggle and grin,
Tickling my palm, let the harvest begin!

In a world of mischief, my plants run amok,
Every little sprout adds to my luck.
I swear if they talk, they'd ask for a sip,
But I'll just water them, and let them trip!

The Ground Beneath My Hands

They say dirt is dirty, oh let them complain,
I’ve got treasures galore and some laughs to gain.
A universe sprawls from these clumsy brows,
Where a kingdom of ants runs its busy house.

Occasionally tripping when I bend to explore,
My fingers find nuggets worth shouting for more.
With a trowel in hand, I rule this domain,
And if you were curious, I’m a dirt-king in vain.

The Language of Loam

In a garden where worms like to chat,
The radishes giggle, how silly is that!
They plot and they scheme, with roots on the run,
While the carrots just laugh, soaking up sun.

The daisies declare they're the fashion brigade,
In polka-dot petals, they're never afraid.
But the cabbage, poor fellow, just wanted to grow,
Yet he's outdone by a plant with a glow.

Textured Terrain of Existence

A patch of mud wears its shoes with finesse,
While the daisies are busy in dress for success.
The critters are gossiping, sharing their woes,
About how the sun gives too many sunburned toes.

The ants hold a meeting to share their grand plans,
With snacks made from crumbs and tiny juice cans.
The grass just rolls over and laughs with delight,
As the bugs put on plays under soft moonlight.

An Offering of Earthy Remembrances

A plant pot conspired with a mischievous seed,
They dreamed of adventures, oh what a wild creed!
Though rooted in place, they'd still reach for the sky,
While the tomatoes just blushed, oh my, oh my!

The cacti weave tales of prickly romances,
Meanwhile, the herbs plot some fragrant advances.
The radish sniffed loudly, claiming the crown,
But he’s no match for that peach tree of brown.

Graffiti of the Green World

The ivy climbed high, it colored the wall,
While the broccoli booed—just not up for it all.
The roses took selfies, all filtered, of course,
While the potatoes rolled eyes at their growing discourse.

The weeds threw a party, inviting the flies,
Their dance moves were wild, oh, it brought the surprise!
But the pansies just sighed, they couldn't relate,
They blossomed in silence, like true garden mates.

Touching Roots and Dreams

Digging deep, I find my prize,
A worm that wiggles, twirls, and sighs.
It looks at me with wide, big eyes,
I swear it plots its own surprise.

My hands are dirty, feels like bliss,
I made a friend, just like this!
We share our dreams of green, of bliss,
He says, "Let’s drag the garden’s kiss!"

Harvesting the Essence of Life

Planting laughs with every seed,
Each sprout is born from my good deed.
I chase the weeds like they're a creed,
They run away, like they can't be freed.

Tomatoes blush under the sun,
I swear they giggle, having fun.
Their juicy jokes have just begun,
With every bite, the laughter's spun.

The Earth's Gentle Caress

In the garden, I dance and sway,
The dirt hugs back, it's here to stay.
With shovel in hand, I find my way,
To plant some humor in this play.

A sunflower nods, it's quite the bro,
It whispers secrets, soft and slow.
"Let's throw a party, let's steal the show!"
Together we bloom, with a bright hello!

Beneath My Touch

With a scoop and dig, I feel alive,
A bug just jumped, oh, what a dive!
It joins the party, what a thrive,
This earthy dance, we all contrive.

The carrots giggle, they're quite the team,
Rooting for laughter, it's their supreme!
Together we plot, we chase the dream,
The garden's magic is a flowing stream.

Life Awakens

In the plot where mischief hides,
Life awakes, with smiles and tides.
The radish rolls, it slyly glides,
While beetroot blushes, laughs it bides.

I dig for treasure, find a shoe,
What once was lost, now feels like new.
I plant my jokes, they sprout and grew,
This garden's the stage for my funny crew!

A Texture of Life

I dug a hole to plant a sprout,
My hands got dirty, there's no doubt!
I thought of gloves, so neat and fine,
But chaos ruled when I crossed that line.

Worms wriggled past, they seemed like friends,
I said, "Hey guys, let’s make amends!"
They looked at me with blank-eyed glee,
Saying, "More dirt? Oh joy! Let’s see!"

Kissed by the Ground

I kissed the earth, it kissed me back,
With muddy lips, just as I lack.
My kids all giggled, couldn't resist,
For planting time brings a muddy twist.

A pot of daisies, sweet and bold,
Turned into a mess; oh, the joy to behold!
My family laughed, “Oh what a scene!”
As I slipped and tripped, it was pure routine!

Handprints in the Earth

I made my mark, what a grand plan,
Then gophers laughed at my brand-new tan!
I dreamed of gardens lush and green,
But ended up knee-deep in a muck machine.

My handprints etched in nature's page,
A masterpiece born from pure outrage!
The neighbors peeked, eyebrows on high,
Said, “Look at that fool, oh my, oh my!”

The Grain of Existence

In tiny grains, life's wonders lie,
But oh, the dust! Oh me, oh my!
Each shovel-full brings gales of laughter,
As I dream of harvests, happily ever after.

My hat flies off, caught on a breeze,
Now I'm chasing it, feeling quite the tease!
With each little giggle, life feels just right,
And dirt is my crown, oh what a sight!

Molding Memories

In the garden, a trowel's game,
Digging deep with a silly claim.
My hands get dirty, oh what a sight,
But the laughter blooms, oh what delight!

A worm winks up, it tickles my palm,
“Hey there, buddy, just stay calm!”
I chuckle loud, as it wriggles around,
Life's little moments, in muck I’ve found.

Textural Tales of the Ground

Fingers squish through a messy patch,
The gooey feel, quite the match!
With every squabble of grit and clay,
I craft a fortress that's here to stay.

Tiny critters start a parade,
"What on earth is this, a muddy brigade?"
They march in style, quite unrefined,
In my hands, their antics unwind.

Presence of the Plant

Greens peek up, all shy and meek,
I say hello, they squeak and squeak!
With fingers dancing in muck so thick,
I chat with daisies, they just giggle quick!

A sunflower leans, with a cheeky wink,
"Dude, you smell like the last drink!"
I toss my head back, laughter in bloom,
Together we giggle in this garden room.

An Indigo Landscape

In twilight’s glow, I start to play,
My hands become a canvas, hooray!
With shades of blue, I splash and smear,
Creating magic that’s far from sheer.

A mischievous bug with glinting eyes,
Sits on my palm, oh what a surprise!
I laugh and ponder, “A painter’s dream,”
With dirty hands, I’m part of the scheme.

Sculpting the Ground

In the garden, I’m a sculptor,
But it’s only dirt I hold.
I shape a statue of a squirrel,
That looks more like a mold.

My hands are caked with treasures,
Each laugh a little cheer.
I fashioned up a castle,
Too bad, it disappeared!

Worms crawl in my masterpiece,
They claim it’s their domain.
With every squirm and wriggle,
I giggle at the gain.

So here I toil with glee,
A finger-painter grand.
A mud pie for my sister,
She’ll love it—ain't that planned?

From Dust to Dreams

With clumps of muck, I ponder,
What might grow from this heap?
A merry band of carrots,
Or a beanstalk tall and steep?

I sprinkle seeds like candy,
And giggle as I play.
Will I harvest gold instead?
Or maybe just some hay?

Each plant a tiny joker,
With roots that stretch and twist.
They whisper all their secrets,
Of leafy dreams and mist.

So here’s to dirt and laughter,
And dreams that spin and sway.
In life’s great garden patch,
I’ll grow my fun today!

Tales of the Tilled Patch

Once I found a trowel,
Right where the radishes thrived.
But instead of digging deep,
I tripped and nearly dived!

A chicken joined my chaos,
She squawked and flapped about.
I swear she stole my shovel,
That sneaky bird—no doubt!

The crops began to giggle,
As weeds danced in dismay.
Who knew that silly farming
Could brighten up my day?

So here I stand in rapture,
With mud upon my cheeks,
The stories from the tillage,
Are treasures that one seeks.

Eden in the Earth

In this patch of glorious muddle,
I'm the queen of all I see.
With daisies in my crown,
I rule both bug and bee.

My loyal mate, a badger,
Brings snacks from 'neath the ground.
He jokes, "These veggies are yours,
But I'm still the best around."

I water all my flower crowns,
With squirts and splashes grand.
Then ran to chase a butterfly,
But slipped and did a LAND!

Oh, laughter fills the garden,
Amid the blooms so fine.
In this earthy patch of laughter,
Life's a funny, sweet design!

Beauty of the Bountiful

In my garden, carrots wiggle,
Rabbits hopping, they make me giggle.
Tomatoes tumble, rolling down,
While a slug dons a leafy crown.

Basil chats with parsley sprigs,
Calling out, 'Let's do a jig!'
Pumpkins plotting a Halloween scheme,
As I plot my salad dream.

Bees buzzing like they've won the race,
Fluttering round in a honeyed chase.
Dirt on my knees, and laughter loud,
I am the proudest plant parent in the crowd.

Lost in the Loam

Digging deep, I lost my phone,
In the muck, it's made its throne.
Who knew worms could stare so wide,
As I look for my techy side?

When I pulled up a wiggly beast,
I thought, 'Great, that'll be my feast!'
But instead, I found it very rude,
To squirm while I just sought some food.

I shout, 'Hey guys, lend me your eyes!'
'Can anyone spot my prized device?'
They all just wriggled, laughing 'we're free!'
The dirt waved back, saying, 'This is key!'

The Call of the Earth

The ground whispers with a funny plea,
'Get those boots, you'll dance with glee!'
I hear it sing each time I rake,
And giggle when the neighbors quake.

Trowel in hand, I always bend,
The plants laugh, 'This is the trend!'
Water splashes all around,
Even weeds are growing proud!

I swear they're plotting a comical heist,
To steal my garden, oh how they're nice!
But with a shovel, I'll defend my patch,
In this funny war, there's no match!

The Artisan’s Touch

With muddy hands, I craft with flair,
Though often, dirt stains linger there.
Potting plants, with grace I swear,
I might shift some if they dare!

Artistry in every scoop,
Let’s not forget my dancing troop!
The seeds roll ’round like tiny stars,
As my garden becomes the local bazaar.

I sculpt with love and plenty of cheer,
Each sprout a testament, oh dear!
Pots are swirling, colors bloom,
I’m a jolly grower, avoiding doom!

Fragments of a Living Universe

In the garden, I dig deep,
Finding treasures that worms keep,
A carrot wearing goggles, oh my,
Says, 'I'm just here to give it a try!'

The daisies chuckle as I poke,
They whisper, 'Is that a shovel or a joke?'
Gravel giggles, and pebbles dance,
Nature's punchline, nothing by chance.

A rogue radish rolls away,
It shouts, 'I'm off to join the fray!'
As I chase it round the patch,
I trip on roots—a perfect match!

The sun grins down with a beam,
While I plot my next comedic scheme,
In this living universe of mine,
Even dirt can be quite divine!

Between the Veins of the Earth

Beneath my feet, a party rages,
In the dark, the critters write pages,
A worm is the DJ, spinning thick,
Beetles breakdance, and ants just click.

I dig and find a snazzy shoe,
Someone lost it—what to do?
'No feet left, but I'm a star!'
Said the sad sneaker, bizarre and ajar.

The moles wear glasses, reading maps,
While roots hold meetings and take naps,
I stand confused with my little spade,
In this underground charade, I wade.

Each shovelful reveals new sights,
I laugh with nature on these nights,
In this soil with wild surprises,
Lies the humor nobody realizes!

Textures of Time and Growth

Rubbing dirt on my old jeans,
Fleeting thoughts of plants and dreams,
As seeds giggle in their small beds,
'Let's sprout, but not in our heads!'

A cactus whispers, 'I'm the best!'
While I ponder my garden quest,
Peas in a pod, they gossip loud,
Hoping one day they'll make me proud.

Tiny sprigs in a grand embrace,
Roaming the garden, it's a race,
While a twig offers sage advice,
'Slow down, my friend, it's quite nice.'

Time to prune, but they all protest,
'Save us the trouble, we're doing our best!'
In this patch of laughter and cheer,
Each texture reveals the joy I hold dear.

The Comfort of the Crust

The crust so warm, a fresh creation,
Mother Nature’s proud foundation,
I squash a bug—oops, didn’t mean!
It was reviewing my gardening scene!

The weeds rebel, they plot and scheme,
'No more tomatoes, we’ll spoil the dream!'
Rocks roll away, the sun starts to tease,
'Join us for fun, we’ll plant some trees!'

I craft my plot with joy and cheer,
While laughter fills the atmosphere,
The roots are jamming in a row,
I sing along, ‘Let’s start the show!’

So here I am, all muddied yet fine,
Each clump of earth a laugh divine,
Amidst the moss, I find my peace,
In nature’s crust, my joys increase!

Harvest Moon's Legacy

Under the moon, the farmers dance,
With a grin so wide, they take a chance.
Turning dirt into glorious gold,
The secret's out, or so I'm told.

With a shovel stuck in the air so high,
They raise a toast to the carrots nigh.
Planting a joke, they pull a weed,
Laughter grows with every seed.

Hats flipped sideways, they strut about,
Worms in pockets, there's no doubt.
They call it mulch, it's just plain mess,
But give it time, it's bound to impress!

As the sun sets low, they tip their hats,
Exchanging tales with the friendly rats.
With the harvest near, they share a cheer,
Farming's a blast, let's have some beer!

Wonders of Native Earth

In the garden, things go splat,
Who thought the turnips would look like that?
Sunflowers towering like giants tall,
But what's that smell? Oh dear, a fall!

A wiggle of worms, a laugh so loud,
They're wriggling out, feeling quite proud.
"Catch me if you can!" they tease and dive,
While I just stand here, trying to thrive.

With boots too big and gloves askew,
I dig for gems but find a shoe.
Curly greens wave from their leafy bed,
"Next year, I'll plant a little less red!"

Under the sun, with giggles abound,
The weeds are winning—what a showdown!
Yet, in this chaos, the joy erupts,
For in this mess, true life erupts!

In the Cradle of the Land

In the cradle of the land, I kneel,
Worms in bowties, a grand deal.
They wriggle, giggle, in the muck,
Fashion shows with nary a truck.

Beetles spin like tiny tops,
While ants march on, no sign of stops.
“Oh dear!” I laugh, “Where's my shoe?”
Looks like it’s gone; I’m feeling blue.

The grass whispers secrets at my feet,
A ticklish joke, oh what a treat!
The sun is shining, my shirt’s a mess,
Nature’s party? I must confess!

But in the chaos, there's a charm,
Plants with jokes, they mean no harm.
I’ll plant my dreams in this funny patch,
Where laughter and roots always match!

The Pulse of the Undergrowth

Beneath the surface, things do thrum,
A hidden rhythm, a dance so dumb.
Frogs on drums start to croak,
With a chorus line made of oak.

Tiny critters in a hurry dash,
Chasing after crumbs in a mad splash.
“Hey you!” I shout, “Have a seat!”
But they just wiggle and retreat.

I'm twirling now on squishy ground,
With every step, I hear a sound.
A turtle laughs and takes its time,
While I’m hopping like I’m in a mime.

A root tickles me, I can’t resist,
With nature's humor, I can’t be missed.
A symphony hidden beneath my toes,
In this leafy world, laughter grows.

Grounded by Nature

Grounded here, my pants are stained,
Little bugs think I'm entertain'd.
"Join the circus!" I hear them say,
As crickets jump in their own ballet.

One ladybug says with a grin,
"You'll never guess where to begin!"
I reply with a playful scoff,
"Is it with this dirt that's on my jacket off?"

The grass beneath starts to chuckle,
As squirrels point and huddle.
"Oh look!" they say, "What a sight!"
Me tangled in vines, what a fright!

Yet in this muddle, I'm full of cheer,
With nature's fun, I have nothing to fear.
A dance on the floor made of clay,
Each mishap brings sunshine to play!

A Dance of Earth and Skin

With arms wide open, I take a dive,
Into the muck where the slugs thrive.
A dance of earth, it's a slippery show,
Every step taken, more laughter in tow.

The daisies giggle with soft delight,
As mud splatters under the sunlight.
"Oops!" I yell, "What a grand splash!"
While worms groove to a squishy bash.

In this garden, where joy meets the ground,
A symphony's born, not a single sound.
Watch me trip over my own two feet,
While ladybugs roll in a radiant heat.

So here I stand, a messy parade,
Wearing my dirt like a funny cascade.
Nature's costume, oh what a win!
In this quirky dance of earth and skin!

Seeds of Connection

In the garden, I stick my hand,
Worms wiggle, oh isn't it grand?
A tomato's hat tipped to the sun,
Saying, ‘Hey friend, let’s have some fun!’

Poking fingers in messy clay,
The radishes roll, and the carrots say,
‘What are you doing? You’re quite a sight!
Digging for treasures in morning light!’

Seedlings gossip about their fate,
‘Will we be salads or on a plate?’
As I chuckle and fluff up the ground,
In this silly patch, joy has found.

With each scoop, a giggle erupts,
Watch out for those bugs that interrupt!
They waddle to chat, my funny crew,
In this vibrant world, there's always a view.

Embracing Earth’s Legacy

In the garden, a dance they do,
Beans twirl, and peas say ‘Whoohoo!’
The daisies wear their evening gowns,
While daisies creak like old-time clowns.

I trip on gnomes in a fashion show,
Leaping o'er onions all in a row,
‘Excuse me, sir, you’re blocking my light!’
Says the pumpkin, all puffed up, what a sight!

A beet sings a tale of his rise,
From humblest duties to sweet surprise,
While I laugh at the antics around,
Nature's comedians wear smiles profound.

With a trowel and smudge on my cheek,
Gardening lessons come bold, not meek,
I promise you this, with each little sprout,
Life’s hard to take seriously, without a doubt!

Earth's Embrace

In my boots, I bounce like a frog,
Thumbs in the dirt, I'm a bit of a hog,
'What are you planting, oh gardener brave?'
Squash with a wink, 'We'll dance in a rave!'

A dandelion joins with a twisty flair,
While a gopher complains it's not fair,
'My tunnels are vast, I should get a feast!
But those pesky roots, I consider a beast!'

With squished berries stuck on my nose,
I laugh at the pie my friend bravely chose,
'A berry blunder,' floral aromas around,
The earth's silly jokes always astound.

In muddy shoes, I leap with delight,
Butterflies giggle, what a delight!
The flora and fauna dance in the breeze,
Imitating me, with graceful ease.

Whispers of the Ground

When the sun peeks out and greets the day,
The ground chuckles softly, ‘Come out and play!’
I scrunch my toes in the cool, dark loam,
And think to myself, ‘Welcome home!’

The cabbage rolls over, laughing out loud,
‘Join the party, you can be proud!’
A hen struts by with a pompous air,
‘Look at my feathers, beauty so rare!’

As I dig deep for a hidden snack,
A potato grumbles, ‘Hey, don’t hold back!’
‘But you’re stuck down here; you’ll never grow,’
The carrots yell, ‘Hey, are we in a show?’

Each plant sways, tells tales so grand,
Of rain that tickles and warm tender hands,
I chuckle at nature’s funny parade,
In this vibrant life, joy is displayed.

In the Grip of Fertile Earth

I scooped up a handful, what a sight,
A worm wiggled, oh what a fright!
With my fingers all muddy, I just grin,
Turns out gardening's where the fun begins.

I found a beetle, dressed in black,
He looked quite regal, what a knack!
As I dug deeper, right on cue,
A toad jumped out, said "Howdy-do!"

With each clump of dirt, discoveries arise,
Tiny treasures, oh what a surprise!
In my quest for blooms, I just can't stop,
This earthy adventure makes my heart hop!

So here I am, a soiled delight,
Cackling with joy, what a silly sight!
For every muck-up, a giggle we'll share,
In the grip of nature, life’s just a fair!

Echoes of Ancient Tillage

In the garden, I wield my spade,
Hoping for veggies to serenade.
A carrot peeked up, looking bold,
And whispered, "You're digging like you’re told!"

I chuckle and snicker at my weedy foes,
Pulling them out as the laughter grows.
With each tug and pull, my hands all stained,
Who knew this dirt play was so well-mannered and trained?

'Twas once a grave for the weeds of yore,
Now my fingers dance, waging friendly war.
With insects buzzing in my ear, oh dear!
Are they my friends or just laughing near?

So I plant my seeds, hope they don’t flop,
With each little sprout, I feel the heart throb.
And when harvest comes, oh what a scene,
I’ll clean up the mess — yes, that’s a routine!

Nature’s Canvas on My Palms

Oh, look at my hands, a painting gone wrong,
Blobs of brown paint, nature's own song.
With splatters of life slung on my shirt,
Artistic endeavors, amidst all the dirt!

Fingers painted in nature's fair play,
A masterpiece crafted, in my own way.
The daisies laugh, the tulips wink,
As I dabble in color, and blossoms think.

My neighbors peek over, confused yet amused,
Wondering how I got so totally screwed.
"Is it a trend?" one politely asks,
As I dig in the dirt, abandoned my tasks!

With mud in my nails, I created this mess,
But oh, what a joy! I couldn’t care less.
Nature's art isn’t clean, nor should it be,
Each splash tells a story, just wait and see!

Moments with Mother Nature

Oh, Mother Nature, what a show,
You toss me clods where'er I go!
My fingers squish, oh, what a game,
Planting a seed, it’s never the same!

The sun on my back, a blister or two,
The weeds plot revenge, it's true, it’s true!
But in a fit of giggles, I start to laugh,
The more I dig, the funnier the gaffe!

With every flower, a joke is born,
The daisies are laughing, the roses adorn.
I shuffle and slip, with a slip and a slide,
With dirt in my hair, there’s no place to hide!

So here we are, in this loony ballet,
With Mother Nature guiding the fray.
Amidst the chaos, I find my bliss,
In the mud-filled moments, nothing’s amiss!

Carefree in the Clay

In the garden, feeling spry,
Backwards somersaults, oh my!
With mud pies flying, dogs in tow,
Turns out, it's quite the show.

Worms wiggling, tickling toes,
Who knew dirt could be so close?
Planting dreams as shadows lay,
The sun is here, hip-hip-hooray!

Pants all stained, a muddy win,
Mom's laughter is the best din.
Giggling with each slip and fall,
Nature's giggles, the best call.

Friends join in, let's make a mess,
Each muddy patch, a sheer success.
So carefree, let worries fade,
Here in clay, the fun is made.

The Language of Earth

A little dance with clods of dirt,
Every step is filled with flirt.
The earth and I, a crafty pair,
Whisper secrets, light as air.

With squishy sounds beneath my shoes,
I wiggle toes and share my news.
The flowers giggle, the grasses sway,
As earthworms cheer, we laugh away.

A high-five with a bumpy stone,
Who knew the ground could be so prone?
To jokes and jests, a jokester's throne,
In every hole, a funny bone.

Grasshoppers hop, they join the cheer,
Nature's crowd, it's loud and clear.
The pitter-patter's quite absurd,
With every laugh, we speak the word.

Chasing the Green

Running wild, my shoes are fate,
I chase the weeds, they think they're great!
A hop, a skip, in sunny rays,
Each sprout taunts me in playful ways.

Dandelions wink, oh cheeky things,
With every bloom, new laughter springs.
I dash and dive, a caper spree,
With nature's pranks, it's wild and free.

Bugs join in, they shimmy and twirl,
In this green dance, I give a whirl.
Butterflies giggle, the breeze on cue,
A playful chase, just me and you.

From clover patches to leafy shrouds,
I frolic free among the crowds.
Green's the color of foolish delight,
In this joyful chase, the world's alright.

Resonance of Roots

In the quiet, roots resound,
Whispers of mischief underground.
They chuckle softly, a giggly crew,
Root parties, and twirling too.

With every shake, a tickling friend,
Holding on tight, they won't transcend.
The trees all blush, their leaves are bright,
As roots plan mischief, out of sight.

Each tiny shoot, a hidden jest,
"Find us here, we're on a quest!"
They wriggle deep, like marionettes,
In nature's game, no regrets.

From underfoot, the laughter rings,
Roots speak the tales of silly things.
A subterranean chuckle floats,
In nature's heart, humor coats.

Hands in the Hearth

In the garden, laughter spreads,
With mud on faces, dreams in beds.
We dig and dance, what a sight!
Who knew dirt could bring so much delight?

A worm wriggles, gives a glee,
As we chase bugs, wild and free.
The sun may shine, the clouds may brood,
But we're the kings of messy mood!

Fingers sticky, they wave and twirl,
Amidst the mess, our thoughts unfurl.
A potpourri of mud and cheer,
In this patch, we shed our fear!

So here's to hands that dig and play,
Turning dirt into a cabaret.
With every scoop, a giggle grows,
In this muddy wonder, joy just flows!

Caress of the Rich Loam

Oh, rich and dark, this wondrous treat,
A slip and slide beneath our feet.
We tumble down, a dirt-clump crew,
Who knew rich stuff could be so goo?

Fingers stained, our faces beam,
In earthy mud, we find our dream.
Beware the splatter, oh my dear!
Laughter echoes, the vibe is clear!

As petals fall, our antics rise,
A garden shenanigans surprise.
With every stroke, a comedy,
Making a mess in harmony!

Funny hands that shape the land,
A band of joy, so unplanned.
In the grit, we find our bliss,
A messy hug, a funky kiss!

Digging Dreams

With every shovel, laughter spills,
We unearth ticks and playful thrills.
'This pocket treasure!' we proclaim,
As mud can fame, not bring us shame.

The plants, they giggle as we dive,
In our dirt castle, we feel alive.
Each clump we toss, a chance for cheer,
What’s hidden here? A dinosaur, dear!

Squishy hands that fashion fun,
In our own world, we’re number one!
Digging deep, where dreams take flight,
In the warm earth, oh what a sight!

To dig, to play, to live, to roam,
In dirt, we find our heart and home.
So let it stick, this artistic scheme,
For in this mess, we live our dream!

Seeds of Touch

We play with seeds, a game divine,
Each little pearl, a chance to shine.
With every toss, a seedling's fate,
To grow and dance, a garden state!

My friend, beware the muddy blast,
When planting seeds, oh what a laugh!
A sprinkle here, a flurry there,
We create chaos, without a care!

The laughter blooms, like flowers bright,
As dirt and dreams take endless flight.
With hands that mold and shape the ground,
We craft the joy that knows no bounds!

When seedlings sprout on our wild stage,
We cheer them on, what a great age!
For in each patch, a joke unfolds,
In the world of dirt, we find our gold!

Tactile Reverie

In a garden, I dig and I delve,
My boots are muddy, oh what a swell!
Worms wiggle like they're in a dance,
I giggle, thinking, they're in a trance.

Hands in the muck, what a sight to behold,
I'm fashioning castles—too bold, too bold!
The neighbors all stare, they want to know,
Why my plants are adorned with a playful glow.

With each scoop, I create a new mess,
My new hobby, I must confess,
Compost like gold, it's a funny old thing,
I chuckle aloud, what joy do I bring!

So here I stand, dirt's my best friend,
With pockets of earth, let the laughter ascend!
Creating a patch to picnic and thrive,
Watch out, world! It's a mud pie alive!

The Warmth of Creation

In gloves too big, I toil and I play,
My fingers turn green in a humorous way.
Seeds take their time, one, two, three,
I'm sprinkling dreams of a future tree.

The sun on my back, oh, what a delight,
I trip on the hose—what a comical sight!
Watering can spills, I slip on the grass,
It's a watery dance, what fun—it's a blast!

Frogs leap nearby, critters ready to cheer,
Squishy and slimy, they bring me good cheer.
Each creature I find, I share my grand scheme,
To grow a great jungle—oh, what a dream!

At day's end, I'm a sight to see,
Covered in bits of earth, wild and free.
If someone should ask how I fared through the day,
I'll just burst out laughing, come join for the play!

Essence of the Burdened Earth

My pots are a kingdom, my yard is my throne,
I'm crafting a paradise, but now I'm all grown!
But wait, what's this—a pesky old weed?
A battle of wits, oh, it's quite a speed!

A trowel in hand like a knight in the fray,
With each tug and pull, I chuckle away.
My adversary laughs as I fumble the fight,
But with one final yank, what a glorious sight!

I plant with the grace of a clumsy ballet,
Spraying myself silly, what a quirky display!
Each root I coax, it grows like a friend,
In this wacky garden, there's laughter to lend.

Bugs buzzing around, have come for the show,
They join in the fun, oh, what do they know?
With soil on my nose, I dance with pure mirth,
In the essence of all that is burdened by earth!

Nurtured by Nature's Hand

Trowel in hand, with a wink and a grin,
I’m on a grand quest, let the chaos begin!
Smudges of earth make a fashionable flare,
My apron’s a canvas—I’ll plant without care!

Sprouting ideas like greens in the patch,
I chat with the flowers—what a fun match!
Petunias gossip, while daisies attest,
In this riot of color, I’m feeling the best.

Digging up laughter, as I sow my delight,
The crows join the chorus, oh what a sight!
Watch me twirl, as I’m planting in cheer,
Each seed a new chuckle that blooms ever clear.

At dusk, with my bounty, I laugh at the sun,
Playing with nature is simply good fun.
With dirt on my chin and joy in my heart,
In this garden of giggles, I’ve played my best part!

The Weight of the World

I dug a hole for my next snack,
Found a worm with an attitude, in black.
"You've got the weight of the world, my friend,
But I think you've just found the bend!"

Every shovel's a secret to share,
With grumpy moles slinking with flair.
They claim my lunch is a fine affair,
But I swear they don't even care!

Then I tripped on a root, oh what a sight,
Roses laughing with all of their might.
"You've lost your balance, don't give up the fight,
Just grab my petals, they're soft and light!"

At the end of my dig, I found a stash,
Of old garden gnomes, oh what a clash!
With a wink and a grin, they gave me a thrash,
'Next time bring snacks, we'll keep it brash!'

Grooves of the Ground

The ground's got grooves like a funky beat,
Each wiggle a dance, oh how sweet!
Earthworms busting moves, ready to greet,
In this boogie of muck, who can't take a seat?

Ants are a conga line, marching in style,
With tiny hats on their heads, all the while.
They wink and they jiggle, they make me smile,
In their underground club, it goes for a mile!

I plopped down to join in the fun,
But my rear end got stuck, oh what a run!
The worms gave me tips, "Just wiggle and stun!"
And soon I was jiving, no longer the pun!

But as I grooved, I made quite a mess,
With soil on my clothes, I surely confess.
They laughed with delight, it was truly a fest,
In the grooves of the ground, was no time for stress!

Fingers Tracing Phosphor

I reached for the ground, in search of a gem,
Instead, found a rock made of bad diadem.
"You call that a treasure? You must be from them,
Where sparkles and dirt mix like a bad emblem!"

Fingers tracing paths like I'm a great artist,
But all I create is a dugout of aist!
A masterpiece made of mud, oh the hardest,
And my critics—the worms—oh, how they're the smartest!

"Dear fingers, you're smudging my glorious base!"
Said the carrot with pride, wearing an orange face.
I giggled too hard—it's no race,
When your art is mischief and you're covered in lace!

It's a garden in chaos, a real uproar,
With laughs of the veggies, they cheer even more.
My fingers like wands, conjure life to explore,
In the land of the roots, I can't help but adore!

The Clay’s Confession

The clay told me secrets it simply can't hide,
Of thumbprints and giggles, all trapped inside.
"I’m a molded rebel, not just a divide,
I’ve held all your mess, now I’m filled with pride!"

Being shaped into pots must sure be a blast,
With flowers on top, they’ve got style that’s vast.
“Just don’t call me dirt, that joke’s overcast,
I’m classy, I’m sassy, I’m made to last!”

But the wind whispered tales of a wild showdown,
With raindrops and mudslides come steal my crown.
"You think you’re the boss, but come on, sit down,
I’m the grand ruler, my grief’s turning brown!"

So I chuckled along, as we swirled in the mire,
With laughter and grit set my heart on fire.
The clay’s life of fun—there's nothing I require,
Just join in the chaos, and let dreams conspire!

Embracing the Untamed

I dug a hole for my new friend,
A worm with a name that's hard to defend.
He wriggled and jiggled, quite out of style,
Said, 'You're in my territory, stay for a while!'

With dirt on my face and grass in my hair,
I pondered if I’d really made a fair share.
The crabgrass laughed, in a verdant hue,
While rabbits chewed clover as if on queue!

My hands got busy, but what’s this mess?
A beetle in pajamas, I must confess!
'You’re late for the party, it’s all the rage,
Come join us right here, hop out of that cage!'

As night draped the garden in shadows and glee,
The slugs did the tango—there's room for all, you see!
With laughter and chaos, the wild took its claim,
Embracing the untamed, all parts of the game!

Caressing the Wild

In a patch of green where the sun met the moon,
I found a chipmunk with a penchant for tunes.
He danced on my garden, shaking his tail,
Squeaking out rhythms while I told my tale.

The daisies chimed in with a petal parade,
While crickets played backup, a tune they had made.
I clapped my dirty hands to the beat,
Joining the chorus, we couldn't be beat!

Messy and merry, the earth seemed to cheer,
As grasshoppers leaped, filling air with good cheer.
My thumbs got stained, a curious sight,
Guess fingers were meant to be wild and bright!

A rock dove by wearing a crown made of weeds,
He called me the ruler of eccentric seeds.
With laughter, we knew, in this garden so mild,
Nature's own magic, caressing the wild!

Whispers of the Ancient

In a corner of earth where the tales intertwine,
A gopher popped up with a vintage design.
'You think you own this? Ha! What a joke!
I've seen kings and queens, and I'm just a bloke.'

The roots laughed aloud, old friends they'd confide,
'We're the real legends, we stretch far and wide!'
A crow with a crown perched high on a tree,
He squawked, 'This garden is all about me!'

So there I sat, hearing stories of lore,
As bugs brought the popcorn, and ants manned the door.
'Your hands get dirty? Oh, what a thrill!
Welcome to our realm, we fit like a drill!'

With whispers of ancient around every bend,
We gathered our laughter, the worms all (attend!)
In a garden of hilarity, tales spun with zest,
With nature's own antics, I certainly was blessed!

Fingers of Fertility

My fingers dived deep, a bold little trip,
Met a carrot who claimed to be quite the hip!
'If it's tender and green, I’m the one to see!'
He boasts with a flair, but a heaping of glee.

Potatoes joined in, with a grin so wide,
'We grow underground, oh the fun we hide!'
While peppers chuckled, their colors a riot,
'If you want spicy tales, you need to try it!'

A ladybug waltzed, with perfect finesse,
'Such talent you’ve got—let’s throw a big mess!'
I flung mud with joy, it splattered with glee,
Nature’s wild dance, it was just you and me!

So here in this corner, with friends galore,
Each finger a sower, I couldn’t ask for more.
With laughter and sproutings, our circles, they swell,
In a garden of chaos, we all cast a spell!

Sensations of the Untamed

I dug my hands in a muddy heap,
A party of worms began to creep.
They wiggled and squiggled, oh what a sight,
Turning my garden into a wormy fright!

A beetle waltzed by, a dancer so bold,
Claiming the title of earth's finest gold.
I laughed and I cooed at this nature's charade,
Who knew that the dirt was a grand masquerade?

My fingers are stylists, they paint with the earth,
Creating a landscape, a whimsical berth.
With a sprinkle of grit and a dab of some seed,
My backyard's a canvas for nature's misdeed!

Oh, the laughter that bubbles from muck and from clay,
I challenge the flowers to join in my play.
With the sun's golden rays, we're crafting a joke,
In the comedy club where the wildflowers poke!

The Pulse of the Earth's Core

With a squeeze of my fingers, the world comes alive,
Tiny creatures party, it's a five-star derive.
I tickle a mushroom, it giggles, it sways,
Turning my garden into a wild playhouse maze!

The ants form a conga line, marching along,
In the rhythm of nature, they sing their own song.
I joined in their jig, oh what a great laugh,
As one bug tripped up, and then took a small half!

My hands are the drumsticks that tap and that pound,
Creating a symphony under the ground.
With roots as the strings and the leaves as the sound,
A concert of chaos that spins all around!

What wonders unfold in this earthy delight,
With bugs as my bandmates, we rock through the night.
I'm the chief conductor of this jolly spree,
In the orchestra of life, come dance here with me!

Embracing the Grit of Creation

In a gritty embrace, oh what can I find,
A treasure of nonsense, a mess intertwined.
With my hands in the mix, there's joy and a grin,
As I unearth the wonders of chaos within!

A squirrel cheeky-chirped, asking for snacks,
While I served him worms, “No backsies!” he quacks.
With laughter ignited, who knew it could be,
A buffet for critters, such culinary spree!

I sculpt little castles with mud as my clay,
Each tower adorned with the wild things that play.
The raccoon held a feast, a party quite grand,
In the kingdom of tissue I made with my hand!

Joy bubbles and giggles in each clump and each clod,
With each silly gesture, the laughter is broad.
So here’s my confession, my secret unveiled,
In the muck of creation, my spirit has sailed!

Traces of Life in My Palm

In the depths of my palm, a dog’s surprise gift,
With wiggling wiggle worms, oh they sure do shift.
I laughed and I fumbled, what a wild event,
As the dog gave a shrug, “Just think of the scent!”

Each tiny sprout whispers a story untold,
Of critters and creatures, oh if they were bold!
I cradle their antics, a ruckus so sweet,
As they plot their bold heists, right under my feet!

My fingers became magic, they dance in delight,
Weaving through petals in the warm, golden light.
With the ants playing tag and the bees holding court,
My hands tell the stories of nature’s report!

A giggle, a wiggle, a smirk on my face,
As I join in their games, in this playful race.
In the traces of life, oh what joy I can see,
In the wild world of giggles, I feel young and free!

Fingers Run Wild

Tiny worms wiggle with glee,
As I squish them, oh look at me!
Tangled roots, a funny sight,
Planting dreams with all my might.

My hands are superheroes, bold,
With capes made of dirt, rough and old.
Each finger a shovel, it's true,
Digging secrets, ooh, what a view!

Pots and pans become my muse,
With my hands, I'll create a ruse.
Sunshine giggles above my head,
While I dance with things I've wed!

A sprout pops up, it makes me grin,
Dirt plastered on my cheek and chin.
Fingers all messy, I don't care,
Nature's laugh is everywhere!

The Earthy Symphony

In the garden, a concert starts,
Beetles playing tiny parts.
The bass of dirt starts to hum,
While worms jive to the drum!

My fingers conduct with flair,
Mixing muck without a care.
Beverly the broccoli shimmies,
As I dance, the dirt still glimmies!

Every rake and shovel sings,
Tickling daisies with their wings.
Muddied hands in a twist and shout,
That’s what nature’s all about!

Harvest moon shines bright tonight,
Compost piles reach new heights.
Fingers swirling, what a tease,
An earthy tune that’s sure to please!

Embers of the Fields

In the field, I start to play,
With dust and dirt, hip-hip-hooray!
A tumbleweed rolls by with style,
And I'm grinning all the while!

My fingers are the architects,
Sketching castles that perplex.
Each crumb tells a tale of cheer,
As spatters dance, not a single fear!

Fluffy clouds above me grin,
While I do a dirt-kid spin.
My hands are covered, who knew?
Flaunting mud like a new tattoo!

Comical crows take a peek,
At my playful, messy streak.
With laughter, I shatter the norm,
In nature's arms, I feel so warm!

Echoes in the Dirt

Giggling roots underfoot,
Ticklish grass that quickly shoots.
Yummy beets hide from my grasp,
But I'll catch them with a laugh!

In the garden, it's pure delight,
With every clump and every bite.
My fingers wiggle, tickling weeds,
While they shout out their funny deeds!

Puddle jumping, muddy flair,
Nature's chaos everywhere.
A rabbit hops with comedic grace,
As I tumble, laughing in place!

Echoes of mischief fill the air,
With every scoop and playful dare.
My hands in the mix, what a treat,
In whispers of dirt, I find my beat!

The Feel of Fresh Growth

I dug in the dirt, what a curious feel,
Worms wiggled and squirmed, oh what a squeal!
I thought I could plant, but found quite a mess,
A carrot? A turnip? I just couldn't guess.

My neighbors all laughed as I stumbled around,
With lettuce on my head, I was garden-bound!
The radishes giggled, they rolled with delight,
My fingers a canvas in pure earthy fight.

But every mistake is a lesson, I know,
The joy of creation, it starts with a show!
I pull out a weed, it's an uninvited guest,
A party in the garden—who knew it was best?

So here's to the chaos of growth all around,
With dirt on my cheeks, I feel quite profound!
I'm planting my dreams with a sprinkle of flair,
Next time, I'll wear gloves—if I even care!

Hands of the Harvest

With baskets in hand, we prance down the lane,
But watch where you step, or you'll slip in the grain!
I picked up a pumpkin, but tripped on a sprout,
Now I'm wrestling vegetables, what's this all about?

The corn stands so tall, but so stubborn and sweet,
One ear said, 'Come on, you're just here for a treat!'
My friends chuckled loud as I squabbled and fought,
For carrots and lettuce, the battle was hot!

But harvest brings laughter, it's not just the yield,
We dance through the fields, our laughter revealed!
A dance off with radishes, so silly and spry,
We giggle and munch 'til the darkens the sky.

So here's to the fun of collecting our cheer,
With nature as co-star, how could you not cheer?
With dirt on our boots, we fondly confess,
The hands of the harvest invite such happiness.

Breath of the Undercurrent

In the garden's hush, there's a whispering sigh,
A movement beneath, as time flits by.
With fingers in rhythm, a tickling laugh,
I unearth some old shoes—who knew they were trash?

Wiggling my toes, I swear I heard giggles,
From gophers below, performing their riddles.
The worms in the dirt, they throw quite a bash,
'Come dance with us, we promise a splash!'

I found quite a treasure—a relic of fun,
A shovel-shaped scepter, for tasks I have done!
I crowned a young sprout as my loyal aide,
Together we conquered, my garden parade.

With dirt on my nose and a grin ear to ear,
I've made many friends in this burly frontier.
Each laugh in the soil, a memory made,
In the breath of the undercurrent, we play!

Life in the Darkness

Under the moonlight, the garden awakes,
A party of critters, oh what a mistake!
I tiptoed through rows, in my boots of bright green,
But tripped on a toad who then made a scene.

The beetles were dancing, all groovy and loud,
'Join us!' they beckoned, 'Come one, gather 'round!'
The cabbage was swaying, in sync with the stars,
With dirt on my shirt, with joy, not with jars.

I pondered to plant in the dark of the night,
But carrots kept snickering, 'You're doing it right!'
The moon was my flashlight, my buddy so bright,
While night bugs conducted the orchestra's might.

So here's to the giggles in midnight's embrace,
With dirt from my antics, I'm winning the race!
In life's quirky shadows, we laugh and we dance,
Who knew that at night, the garden's romance?

In the Heart of Creation

With dirt on my palms, I make a mess,
My garden's a comedy, I must confess.
The veggies are wild, the flowers ask why,
As I chase a lost worm that wiggled by.

My neighbor just giggles, says I'm quite a sight,
With pants full of mud, I'm a true delight.
I planted a pumpkin, but got a squash,
Now I'm baking bread with a vegetable nosh.

The bugs are my buddies, we chat and we play,
They tell me their secrets in such a weird way.
A ladybug laughed, said she's on a diet,
I offered her lettuce, but still, she won't try it.

Through rakes and spades, I wonder and roam,
In my tiny patch, I've built a small home.
With laughter and giggles, my garden's alive,
In this wild little world, I'm the silliest hive.

Sculpted by the Seasons

In spring I’m a genius, with shovels and cheer,
Yet autumn brings chaos, my plants disappear.
I dress like a sage, but I’m really a fool,
With my mismatched gloves, I break every rule.

Summer's a party, the daisies all dance,
While cucumbers plot some mischievous prance.
I try to be clever, to grow something grand,
But carrots keep hiding, oh, they’re bad at this plan!

When winter rolls in, I get cozy and bright,
With tea leaves, I giggle at frostbitten bites.
My garden's a puzzle, a comedic delight,
Every day’s a show, oh, what pure delight!

So here's to the seasons, and all that they bring,
A comedy play, where the blooms are the king.
I may not have mastered this planting charade,
But I’ll keep cracking jokes in this homemade parade.

Conversations with Clay

My hands dive in mud, it's a glorious stew,
And pottery whispers, 'Come play, join the crew!'
A bowl says, "Make me, for soup or for pie,"
I trip on the wheel, and pots laugh nearby.

With every wild spin, I'm a clay-slinging king,
Yet my mugs keep flopping, oh, what a fling!
The owls in the room hoot a hooty delight,
As I sculpt my creations with charm and with fright.

"Just try to be steady!" a teacup then shouts,
While I'm here like a clown, full of mud and doubts.
A teapot gives sass, says she's seen better days,
Yet here I'm a jester in wholesome clay plays.

In this mess of my making, I'm laughing out loud,
With clay underfoot, I'm quite the proud crowd.
To shape dreams in dirt feels like whimsy in pairs,
Each piece tells a story, through giggles and stares.

The Earth's Serenade

The ground has a rhythm, a dance of pure fun,
As I dig up my dreams with a spoon and a pun.
The daisies are singing, the worms join the show,
I'm the great maestro, watch my garden grow!

I've got onions for trumpets and radishes too,
While carrots do tango in a vibrant hue.
The sunflowers swing, waving high in the breeze,
While I take my bow, covered in dirt with ease.

The apples are munching on sweet laughter's crunch,
As I twirl past the lettuce, they say, "Let's have lunch!"
With each bend and twist, oh, what a weird tale,
My garden's a symphony, where giggles prevail.

So come take a visit, grab a shovel and play,
Join in this concert, where dirt rules the day!
In this whimsical world, I'm the jester, not wise,
But with laughter and green thumbs, we'll reach for the skies!

www.ingramcontent.com/pod-product-compliance
Lightning Source LLC
Chambersburg PA
CBHW070322120526
44590CB00017B/2778

CONTENTS

small change

PART 1
Preamble

PART 2
General Proceedings

PART 3
a biography (in three voices)

PART 4
Epilogue

PART 5
The Glossary of Terms and Phrases

PART 6
Afterwords

small change

Introduction

In August 2024, the Creative Practice Circle (CPC) of Charles Sturt University (Australia) conducted a weeklong workshop event in Wagga Wagga, New South Wales, with attendees traveling in person or participating via Zoom link-up.

The theme for this weeklong retreat was *Cries from the Anthropocene* and the CPC invited creative, scientific and research specialists to make presentations of their work and current findings to assist the CPC in addressing its goals for the retreat, which were:[1]

- How might the arts intersect with the grief and anxiety of living in the Anthropocene?
- What is the role of creative practice as a research methodology for exploring fear and loss?
- What opportunities exist for interdisciplinary engagement between artists, humanities scholars, scientists, activists and environmental experts in engaging with our theme?
- What opportunities exist for working with diverse cultural communities and Indigenous peoples?
- How can we amplify our voices when it seems that nobody (that is, nobody in power) seems to be responding with a sense of urgency congruent to the known facts of the climate emergency?
- How might we account for and acknowledge the more-than-human world, and/or that of the Unknown Other – those we can't see or hear because we don't recognise them?

---

1 *https://creativepracticecircle.csu.domains/research—themes/cries—from—the—anthropocene/research—theme—2024—2025/*

- The meaning of silence – indifference? disagreement? pain? – can seem mysterious. How do we interpret silence from the human and more-than-human worlds in the face of the Anthropocene?

small change represents the response of one attendee to what he saw and heard. Thought and felt.

The collection is comprised of interpretative stories told in free verse poetry from a range of points of view, because that is what I, as a poet/storyteller do.

Frank Prem
2025

PART 1

Preamble

retreat (to wagga)

the man
working the coffee van
warns me

kangaroos!

~

it is pre-dawn
and a coffee '*traveller*'
will be a boon
on a long journey

coffee-man is right
of course

the kangaroos
have been numerous
and the consequences
of striking one
while on the road
are appalling

dead or damaged roo

dead or damaged vehicle

general distress

~

as I leave town
my '*traveller*' safely ensconced
in a cup-holder
I move
at a crawling pace
through thick fog

my mind wanders
to touch memories and rumours
of other obstacles
that might lie
in the path
of an unsuspecting journeyman

fallen trees
have been frequent

koalas and echidnas
crossing where
they should not

kangaroos and wallabies
yes
but the most recent trauma
has been deer

for months
there have been reports
of a big sambar buck
haunting the verges
of the road to our nearest
large town —
the city of wodonga

more recently
reports have come in
of a whole troop
of them
looking to cross
from one side of the road
to the other
in front of traffic

deer
are bigger
than kangaroos

~

in the event
it is ducks

a small flock
of wood ducks
settled in the middle
of the road

straddling the centreline
before a flurry
of panic and wings
explodes them
into the air

a near-invisible hazard
avoided only because
I am crawling so slowly
with the headlights
of another car
shining up my clacker

too close
for too long

~

the journey
is rapidly becoming
an eternity
adorned in pearl and silver

~

from the sides of the road
phantom trees
loom at me

some
are skeletally dead things
caught in mid-gesticulation

pointing everywhere

nowhere

sleek black crows
seem at home
on the ground

all strut
and ruffle

preening glossily
while they wait

fresh roadkill
can’t be far
away

~

the road
wears a gown
of soulless hues

ragged
and dull

enlivened
for a moment
by a flash of light
that suddenly illuminates
as though striking a golden brooch

an adornment pinned
at the shoulder

then
the moment of sunlight
is gone
and I am wreathed dull
again

~

culcairn
is nothing but a trap

my plan is to travel
by main road
to wagga

the sign at culcairn
suggested
I turn off to the right

now I find
that am no longer
on a main road

by the time
I have worked it all out
this is no longer
a straightforward trip
from *point a* to *point wagga*

it is now a rambling day trip
through invisible countryside

~

carparks

number 4

number 5

6

7

a little forward
a little back

the university campus
can only be navigated
by carpark numbers

building names
and their locations
are a secondary level
of signposting
unworthy of highlight

carpark 5

I have arrived

PART 2

General Proceedings

to tell you harder (a scientist's lament)

I try . . .

she said

we *try*
to uncover

to discover
what
we do not know

to find truth
beneath the microscope

or where it hides –
concealed among the data points

we draw maps
to explain
the waveforms
of our universe

and paint the pictures
that reveal
the desperation
of our own demise

I try . . .

she said

we *try*
to explain

then we try
again
this time
a little harder

a little deeper

you . . .

you *are not*
listening

you

you *cannot*
hear

my voice . . .

our *voice*
is a white noise
disturbing friday night

  the evening meal

  the football game

our voice
is a howling wind
that bears no rain

it is the waving heat
that raises vapour
from
a burning land

and shimmers like a mirage
you may choose
to believe in

or not

I will try . . .

she said

we *will try*
to tell you

harder

the uncertainty (could make me crazy)

I know
what I do not know
and I am certain
of my uncertainty

I can plan
my do's and don'ts
for sure

avoid the void
where my knowledge
does not extend

I
can live my life
that way

~

I don't know
what I know
for sure

I don't know
what
I do not know

where it begins
or
where it ends

is it me . . .

is it other . . .

will it harm me . . .

might I break it . . .

I don't know
and
living with this . . .

living *like* this
is going to drive
me
crazy

drawn on the linen (and never the same)

draw me an outline
on linen

a map
to show me
where to go

the river is wide
and
the river
is deep

unroll the cloth

unfold the guide
made for me
especial
by my own sweet bride

a chart

for these waters
flow
never the same

a guide
for the stumbling pilot

and ever-sweet
will be
her name

just one (through the mirror)

I have a mirror
of myself
in *another* place

a *different* where

she walks with me
though *she*
is *there*
and I
am *here*

our footsteps touch down
upon the earth
together

we mark our paths
as though we were
just *one*

I am
a mirror
of someone
in another place

I walk with her
though I
am here

place my feet
when
she places hers

way over there . . .

away
over there

we walk together
as though we are
just one

we two

as though we hold
each other
in a mirror

low water (and hunger stones)

the river falls
like
it has never fallen
before

a drought
that is
the worst of times

the river falls

a rock is exposed
and shows
a letter from
the past

carved letters
from the past

read me and weep
my dears

if
you can read me
then weep

go down upon your knees
my darlings

if you can read me . . .

only god
can help you
now

in a year (I'll save the planet)

who
can save a planet

not me
for I
am small

not me
for I can't see beyond
my dinnertime
(approaching fast)

beyond the toil
I give
to get my pay

not me

for I
am tired today

it's not my task

and not
my job

maybe
on another day . . .

maybe
in a year

a farmer and his paycheck (still waiting)

last year
and
the year before . . .

those years
that followed after covid

we worked our land
and livestock
the best ways
that we could

and sent them off
when they were reared
or
after the harvest
was in

and people
were fed
and clothed

bread
on the table
and milk
in the fridge

we're proud of that
though sometimes
it seems
that no one knows

that no one cares

it all came
from us
here on the land

I don’t like to sound
as though I’m crying about it

nobody around here
would care
to whinge

but no one out there
knows
and no one out there
spares a thought

and me . . .

I’m still waiting
to be paid . . .

something

anything

I can’t make a noise about it
in case the future
is weak
and it’s all built up
on a deck of cards

but a full year’s gone by

then gone by
again

and I’m still waiting
to be paid

a small change (of habit)

I don't do
much

we are talking
as we walk

he pauses
mid-step
to retrieve some small thing –
a wrapper
or a piece of packaging –
which he thrusts
into an over-sized and over-filled
pocket

pushes it down
to ensure
a little room remains
for the next thing

I used to drive
all the time

everywhere

I loved driving
but I stopped

decided that
in a small little
local environment
like mine

I really didn't need
to drive
a car

in fact
I could only justify it
until
I actually stopped
to think about it

it's not
a big thing in itself
but . . .

it took some
getting used to

I gave myself little rewards
for my efforts

like a café coffee
or
a cooked breakfast

an hour of reading and browsing
in the library

small rewards
for small changes

he stopped again
this time to thrust
an arm
deep into a small patch
of bulrushes
growing beside the path
we were walking on

it's marvellous

he said

how
they look
so much better . . .

more
'as intended'
when you've fetched
the rubbish
out of them

it is a small piece
of clear plastic –
some remnant piece
of wrapping –
that he has fished out this time

and

he said

when you do
start to notice . . .

to see things
where they shouldn't be

it becomes
a habit

a small change
of habit

communicating (brain to gut)

Winter too warm? Climate Change!

Feeling the heat?   Global Warming!

I'm just experimenting

a little practice
for when the ad campaign
gets the go-ahead

the scientists
and boffins
have got their hands full
trying to convince the pollies

and they haven't got a hope
of getting
to the *hoi polloi*

the consuming masses
don't want to waste their time
sifting through science

they don't want *facts*

they want *feelings*

emotion
that wrenches their gut

and
they want answers
too

simple answers
and not just questions
and guilt trips

most of all
they don't want to feel
like they have to lose
something
from their lives

scientists can't give them
what they need

they're too smart
and
they're not smart enough
both
at the same time

the job needs an ad agency

Going to the footy? *Catch a Train!*

Take a mate!

Watch it on TV!

a sharp little campaign that uses
six to ten words
max

bounce it at them
from the tv
every evening
as a series of small messages

night after night

relentless

Define the problem. – *Give a solution.*

Express a desire. – *Show a way.*

this stuff isn't
brain to brain communication

it's brain to gut

the problems
have to mesh
with *consumer* awareness

the solutions have to be

I can do that.

That's not too hard.

There's something in this
for me.

save the science
for decision makers with money
in their pockets

and make sure
there's *something in it*
for them
as well

nobody saves the world
for free

New Climate Campaign? *See Twiggy!*

anyway
I've got a call to make

let's see if I can get us
some funds for this campaign

Hello,
is that Mr Forrest?

Thanks for taking my call.
I just wanted to run something
past you . . .

turning grey (conversation with a farmer)

when I was a youngster
I was into
everything

there was no part
of the farm
I didn't know

cropping or sheep
or tractors . . .

they were all the same

my sister emma
was just like me
and I guess
we could be
a bit of a nuisance to dad
sometimes

but he always took the time
with us

he said
that he'd had it hard
from his own father
when he was growing up
and getting that old man
to recognise the need
for change
and to let someone younger
have the space to learn and grow
was near impossible

and convincing him to step back
from running the place
in his own old ways
took a stroke

dad didn't want that to happen
with us

so he'd always thought about
a gradual handover

to let us –
the new generation –
explore our ideas
and renew things

he and mum
would gradually move themselves
out of our road
and we could step up

now though
he's not so sure

there have been
too many years
of poor prices

too many wasted seasons
with no rain

wild dogs
at the lambs
are uncontrollable

so many sambar deer
that they outnumber
the kangaroos

more kangaroos
than sheep
and not enough pasture
to go round them all

he thinks
now
that the farm will be a burden
and that em and me
should just get jobs
in town
and sell the land
to set us up well

there will probably
be enough money for that
if the prices hold

him and mum
could keep an acre
on the corner

a little house
near where the farm –
their whole lives –
had been

they'd still feel a bit
of the same dirt
under their feet
in a
kind of way

but me and em
have been talking

we're a bit torn
about that

we feel like
it should be our dirt
too

we
grew up on it

it runs in our blood

if it's sold
there'll be no-one
to care for it

and
to breathe it
every morning
the way it needs
to be breathed

these are hard times
filled
with uncertainties
and
none of us know
what we should do
or how
we should do it

but it could all change
with one good season . . .

perhaps two

my memories are filled
with farm colours

blue skies

green grass

brown dirt

white sheep

yellow grain

but the days now
all seem to be turning out
grey

no favourites (but blue butterflies)

I try not to pick
favourites

out in the garden –
what I call
my garden –
they should be
all the same

if they blossom
they are beautiful

if they buzz
they're a joy

the pleasure
of flowers
and their insects
is never-ending

yet
I can't help being drawn
more to some
than to others

like a sunflower
that is really hundreds
of flowers in one

honeybees and damselflies

I drill down
even further
though

to the native bees
and hover flies

the little blue lawn butterflies

for the last couple
of years
I've found myself worrying
that the little butterflies
hadn't made an appearance
by the time
I thought they should
before suddenly finding them
everywhere
as springtime progressed

it's a strange thing
because I know
I was probably just not seeing
what was right before my eyes
but
it concerned me

the relief
when I saw them again
was palpable

they're such sweet
little things

so delicate

this year
it is just
the first week
of spring
and I've found them
in numbers

a deeper blue –
near purple –
than what I recall
but
they are certainly about

there is a little
violet-flowering
daisy bush
at one corner of the garden
and it is covered
in them

a perennial bush
that flowers
all through winter

my butterflies
seem to love it

tiny hoverflies
as well

.
.
.

I think
I may need to plant
some more
daisies

it's time
to play
favourites

musing (on a fair go)

do unto others . .

do unto others . . .

they wrote that
into the bible
didn't they

do unto
others
as you'd like them to do
unto you

the golden rule

in australia
we call it
a fair go

an equal chance

being done right
by

I read the news
every day
online
because nobody
does paper
anymore

and I see stuff

interest rates
are too high
so that we can’t afford
to spend

public education
that’s so crap
parents are almost forced
to send their kids
off
to private schools

teachers grooming children
placed in their care
for something other than a degree
in the arts

people needing to get a second job
to pay the mortgage

and a third job
to pay
for childcare

every phone call
is a scam

and the farmers say
they can’t keep going
on what the supermarkets
will pay them
for dairy and beef
chicken
and eggs

vegetables

the world is full
of refugees
all running because somehow
war and despotism
have come back into fashion

none of them
are welcome
in australia

all of them
are a threat
to you and me
because of where
they have come from
and what
has been done to them

around the globe
the oligarchs grow
oligarch-ier

they have so much
but it's not enough

somehow
it can never be
enough

they want to rule the world
while they keep
destroying it

chewing it up

spitting it out

chewing some more

meanwhile
don't anybody –
any one of you
or me –
say a word
against

such divisiveness
is
intolerable

a fair go
they say
is not
for everyone

not for *just*
anyone

a fair go . . .

what does it look
like

what
does it feel like

do you know anyone
who gets one . . .

who
has had one . . .

done to you

done to me

done is done
so don't complain
or
if you do . . .

if you do
well
they'll see you
in court

it's only fair

save what (there is no time)

people that know
say
when the fire
is coming
or
the floodwaters
are rising
and you can't stop them
you should pack a few essentials
and things
you can't live without

then go

get to safety

I wonder –
now that the fire
and the flood
are nearing my doorstep –
what
would I want to take
that I could not live
without

I think
that what I most want
is a photographic memory

to remember the paper daisy
that grows around my local wilderness –
the gorge

it has a flower that is coloured
in soft lemon-gold-red shades
and they are managed
by attendant ants

[SNAP]

while I'm there
I'm reminded of
the nodding greenhood orchids
that appear in springtime
and autumn

[SNAP]

who doesn't love
a koala

we get them
from time to time
wandering a bit forlornly
on the streets

they look cuddly
but sound ferocious
when they're lusting
in the night

who wouldn't love *them*

[SNAP]

there is a creek
that runs
right through the heart
of town

silver by name
and silver it runs

when I was young
I would sometimes fish
for small trout
in it

in reality
I liked to be
on my own

lying back
while concealed on the bank
and having a secret cigarette

a couple of years back
silver creek dried up altogether
because it was overused
upstream
by a commercial worm-farm
of all things

I was devastated

felt that the little world
I live in
had been assaulted

[SNAP]

up amongst
the plantation timbers
a couple of miles
out of town
there is a stand
of sequoia redwoods

they must be
around a hundred years old
by now

these are trees
that don't really belong
around here
but
they are magnificent

folk call them
the magic forest

the air
underneath them
breathes different

it's an amazing thing

[SNAP]

there's more

there is always
going to be
more
that I would like
to save

to take with me
and keep safe

but
the fire is coming

the waters
are rising

we'd better collect them
as best we can
while there is still
a little time

a land of pests (and weeds)

well
you know
about european rabbits
of course

the country's been trying
to get rid of them
for about two hundred
years

we haven't been able to cull them
to extinction
in all that time

they were a sporting idea
at first
but by the early nineteen hundreds
they were a plague
and tucker

people on the farms
and in the towns
wouldn't have survived
if the pesky things
weren't such good breeders

and there's pigs
and goats and horses

camels
buffalo
foxes
cane toads

cats

deer

all introduced
some released
some escaped

all of them quite at home
in the bush
despite the perpetual efforts
at culling them

but that's not all
you mustn't forget
the natives
that are thought of as pests
as well

like kangaroos and wallabies
emus

kookaburras and magpies

cockatoos and wombats
crocodiles and snakes

dingoes too
of course

it's a muddled business

if the government
was serious
about culling these creatures
until they were no longer
a problem
it would be relatively simple

kill them
until there aren't any left

not easy
but
simple in concept

that isn't how
culling works though

the goal of a cull –
which is
killing
of course –
is not eradication of these *pests*

no

the object
is to *control* them

the problem with that
is that the pests
are too smart

or they've got
human supporters

or
they're good food
or good hunting
or . . .

well
you get the drift

you know
it might get to a point
where the pests
that we're trying to manage
for the farmers
and what have you . . .

it *might* get to the point
where it's easier to farm *them*
than it is
to farm the sheep
and the cattle
that are all the go now

so
are you settled in
and comfy . . .

good-o

now
I'll tell you
about the feral weed problem

there's gamba grass
gorse
paterson's curse and blackberry

lantana and . . .

time . . . (. . . emit)

I can't wait for saturday to come it seems to take forever I'll be old before my time . . . before saturday	I can't believe how fast my life has gone it seems like last saturday . . . just last saturday I was young waiting forever for my life to have started
they say that I'll forget that all I need is enough time I hope what they say is true that with time I might forget a broken heart	what do you call that . . . that yellow flower I know it . . . I *think* I know it from its scent it reminds me of something of sometime it is hard to recall when everything forgets

if
we don't act
now

it will be
all over

if we don't . . .

look
there'll be *nothing* left

we will have ruined
every thing
if
we don't act *now*

we are running
out
of time

be calm
be calm

you and I
are not
the only ones

not
the only *things*

we were not
the first

we will not be
the last

if change comes . . .

well
change has come
before

if change comes
it will bring
something

some thing

for tomorrow

post-apocalyptic lunch time (food on the table)

catch
the water
falling from the sky

sprinkle seed for growing
by and by

weeds
for the blender

green drink
to keep you well

what you catch
you can render

it's protein
and you can't really tell

hunt food and gather
that
has always been
the way

if there's anything
left out there
bring it home
today

catch water
gather green things
hunt protein
as you will

put the food
onto the table
that is all there is
until . . .

the god (of the modelling process)

I would like
to *try* . . .

I would like
to *see* . . .

. . . if I make
the clouds
a little thicker
here . . .

. . . add a little
acidity . . .

. . . some Co2 . . .

. . . some other
chemical composition . . .

alkalinity perhaps

to change the rain

the *nature*
of the rain

I wonder what
that
might do . . .

~

hmm

that
was interesting

much death and destruction
of existing flora
and fauna

quite a lot
of extinctions

widespread crop failures
and so on
but
some unexpected positives
from non-dominants

this time . . .

this time
I think I should work
with temperature

if the core
is *increased* in this area
here
in the north . . .

let's say
two degrees . . .

three
perhaps

that should do something
to the ice –
I can make projections
of the impact
quite easily –
but

small change

if I *decrease*
the temperature
in the south
at the *same* time . . .

well
that might produce
some very interesting reactions
at both ends
and in the middle . . .

at the equator

I predict
some extraordinary
storm activity
in the oceans

typhoons and cyclones . . .

weirding of the weather
on land

all right then

nothing for it
but
to find out

PART 3

a biography (in three voices)

1956

past

elvis is top of the charts
and norma jean
has become marilyn

> *for the first time*
> *there is an event*
> *called eurovision*

in australia
the olympics are staged
in melbourne

> *a male baby is born*
> *in hamburg*
> *germany*

1591 mm of rain falls
in beechworth

history

it is the year
that the extended family
leave yugoslavia
to get away
from communism
and find a future

two generations
settle in germany
en route to somewhere else

they share everything

all the adults have work
and
for the first time
in a generation
feel a collective sense
of optimism

memory

I remember nothing
of my babyhood

my mother told me
I had been ill
in my first year of life

mumps

an operation left me
with a soft lump
under the jaw

as a child
I would often explore the lump
with my fingers
and try to work out
if I was deformed
because of it

1961

past

a wall is built
to divide
berlin

a cosmonaut
flies around the earth
then falls to ground
by parachute
while patsy cline
falls to pieces

in australia
lady chatterley
and her lover
are banned

a youngster hides himself
among the flour sacks
in a cupboard under the sink
in the kitchen
as a pleasant game

765 mm of rain falls
in beechworth

history

the family is not able
to stay in germany

they find their way
to australia
by aeroplane

to *beechworth*
near the new south wales border
because there is a relative
already living there

the men find work in the forests

infant frank's mother
finds work
in the local lunatic asylum

other emigre families
and friends
have gone off to the city
to live and work
and to form
a supportive ethnic social circle

the family has no one to rely on
but themselves
and a few souls
from other parts of europe
who ended up in the same place

the same circumstance

memory

I was playing at the house
of an old lady
baby-sitter
with other children
while our parents worked

a shelf
was knocked over

drying onions
fell to the ground
in a scatter of papery brown skins

I ran away
afraid of being blamed
for the mishap

walked a mile and a half
alone
to find my way home

1966

past

an artificial heart
is installed in a human chest
with no
visible emotion

the sound of music
is judged the best
motion picture
of the year

in australia
ten shillings
turns into a dollar
and a dollar
now makes cents

in an act of petulance
a boy
on the way to school –
lobs a rock
over a high fence

strikes his sister
on the head

1144 mm of rain falls
in beechworth

history

the extended family
is now two households –
the younger *george* household
and the older *anton* household –
living in the same town

work
is the driver for all

mental hospital back-wards
for the young mother

mental hospital kitchens
for the young father

and a plumbing second-job

and a grass-hay gathering second-job

and a tobacco-picking second-job . . .

nightly beers at the pub
are the key to getting
the necessary second-jobs
and are responsible
for the arguments
at home

young frank
is riding a bicycle
that has been assembled
by his father

memory

our chookyard was overhung
by a large mulberry tree

below it lay a pit
made for composting
grass clippings and such

the game
was to leap like superman
from the roof
of the adjoining garage

the aim . . .

to land
on top of the grass
inside the pit

not to fall
on the bricked barrier
or roll over it
and into the scattered
chook droppings

1971

past

astronauts
have walked
on the moon
for a third time

evel knievel can jump
over nineteen cars

in australia
the beginning of the end
of its war
in vietnam
is being implemented

an adolescent male is worried
that national conscription –
the 'nasho' –
requiring young men to serve
in the army
will not end soon enough
to save him
from having to fight in the war

1100 mm of rain falls
in beechworth

history

both households
have become well established

there is a plan for the george family
to visit europe next year

germany and yugoslavia

the young mother
would have gone sooner
but was not allowed
to take the children with her
just in case she failed to return

homesickness for her own family
has eaten at her
since leaving germany years ago

a teenaged frank
wears hair to his shoulders

he goes out on the weekends
to drink
secretly and illegally
with friends

smokes cigarettes

grandfather *anton*
buys him an ashtray as a present –
without explanation –
after seeing him with his friends
one evening

memory

dad
bought a super 8
movie camera

it was intended to record
our planned trip to europe
next year

I became the feature
in a test shoot
of the whirring device

captured in my long hair
and a hippy hat

in the movie
I looked efficient
but sullen

reluctantly pushing
the lawn mower
back and forth
across the backyard grass

1976

past

star wars is filming
in tunisia

apple
is a computer

a telephone

a reading device

in australia
the *blue hills* radio serial
has ended
after thirty-two years
on air

a still-teenage beau
is laying the foundations
for marriage

he is not
well prepared

752.8 mm of rain falls
in beechworth

history

the george family
has evolved

the daughter
has gone travelling overseas
working for a tour-bus company

frank is working
as a junior officer
in a bank

he has lived away from home
and returned
and now receives a transfer
to work in melbourne

he has met a special someone
and there is an air of love
around him

an air of lust

by year end
his marriage
has been scheduled

memory

I would travel from melbourne
where I lived then
back to the north-east
every weekend

I'd drive
straight from work
on friday
and into the night
to get there

> *there was a girl*
> *and a sense of –*
> *perhaps –*
> *belonging to something*
> *more than myself*

it was like a hunger

an urgency

1981

past

ronald reagan is shot
but lives

last year
john lennon was
but didn't

> *bob marley*
> *dies*
> *at thirty-six years*
> *of age*

in australia
a baby
taken by a dingo
is the subject of the first
of four public inquests

> *a young husband*
> *and father*
> *is a psychiatric nurse*
> *working in melbourne*

1342 mm of rain falls
in beechworth

history

frank
is a father now
of two children

he moved back to the north-east
from the city
when he married
but his employment soured

he subsequently trained
to become a nurse
at the local psychiatric hospital

he can't understand
the deep unhappiness
and the sense of confusion
that frequently envelopes him

he is finding work
with psychiatric patients
both confronting
and exhilarating

without consulting anyone
he submitted an application
for a nursing job
in melbourne

his application has been successful

memory

without really knowing it
I had been depressed
for a long time

struggling to cope
with my life
and responsibilities

my *family* responsibilities

> *I wanted to run away*
> *and*
> *made my mind up*
> *to do it*
>
> *to move to melbourne*
> *by myself*
> *and disguise what I was doing*
> *as acceptence of a promotion*

I manufactured
an escape

1986

past

after seventy-three seconds
of flight
a space shuttle explodes

the bodies of all seven astronauts
are later recovered

> *the chernobyl*
> *nuclear power station*
> *powers four thousand*
> *deaths*

in australia
the *weeping woman* painting
by picasso
is stolen from a gallery

she is found unharmed
two weeks later
in a railroad storage locker

> *a thirty-year-old man*
> *is a project officer*
> *with a small role in implementing change*
> *within the psychiatric system*

1029 mm of rain falls
in beechworth

history

a re-unified nuclear family
has established itself
in melbourne

> *frank has begun climbing*
> *his career ladder*
> *boosted along*
> *by unionist connections*
>
> *in his work he helps to design*
> *a career and salary structure*
> *for psychiatric nurses*

his father has warned him
prophetically
that he should be sure
to keep his head
down
when the bullets
start flying

memory

in melbourne I became
a small-time activist
within the mental health
department

a project officer
bouncing between jobs and roles

it was all new and exciting
and I was absolutely full of myself
and all the wonderful things
that I could now touch

effect

make happen

good days

1991

past

ukraine and fourteen
other states
vote for independence
from the soviet union

info.cern.ch
is the first website established
on the world wide web

in australia
the world's largest
blue-green algal bloom
takes place on the darling river

an overextended
nurse middle manager
experiences a bout
of weeping
in the bathroom facility
at his workplace

975 mm of rain falls
in beechworth

history

frank
has become
a psychiatric services bureaucrat

his work involves him
in the closure
of the old
and decrepit
state-run lunatic asylums

he staffs a telephone hotline
for disaffected nurses
in the midst of a nasty
state-wide industrial dispute

the circles
under his eyes
are a reflection
of the darkness he absorbs
through the phone

memory

work
had been difficult
for some time

the rotten old loony bins
were corrupt and disgusting
and had to go

the workforce resistance
to change and modernisation
was extraordinary

all day long
during the strike
I was on the phone
talking to and advising distressed nurses
about what they should do
to survive the strike

to relatives and carers
of hospital patients
explaining why their loved ones
were suddenly out on the streets

I was exhausted

the union –
my old union –
had been the subject
of a hostile takeover

it was now
the enemy

1996

past

the ira bombs docklands
at canary wharf
in london

dolly
a cloned sheep
is born in scotland

in australia
a lone gunman shoots
and kills
thirty-five people
in the old convict settlement
of port arthur
in tasmania

a forty-year-old
former bureaucrat
undertakes private consultant work
reporting
on troubled human services

he recommends
plausible solutions
and responses

1313 mm of rain falls
in beechworth

history

frank has left the bureaucracy
and clinical nursing

he is attempting
to forge a career
as a private adviser
in his fields of expertise

a consultant

the work he obtains
is sporadic
and financial despair
is never
very far away

he feels
that he has become
a deeply cynical
and unhappy man
but
can't find an escape
from a near-constant sense
of personal failure
and subsequent despair

memory

consultancy
was interesting work
but very flukey

any downtime –
and there was *far* too much
downtime –
brought worry about money
and survival

> *an equally idle colleague and I*
> *each purchased a half-set*
> *of golf clubs*
> *and spent time*
> *frightening grass*
>
> *swings*
> *and misses*
> *with a driving iron*

I had given up smoking
for thirteen years
but that
was history

2001

past

an al-qaeda attack
on four targets in the united states
claims three thousand lives

the twin towers fall

the first maps
of the human genome
are published

in australia
the *mv tampa*
with a load of refugees aboard
is refused permission
to enter australian waters

a newly divorced
middle-forties man
is prepared to admit publicly
for the first time
that he identifies
as a poet

rainfall data is not recorded
by the Bureau of Meteorology
but

1146 mm of rain falls
in beechworth in 2000

history

frank continues
to make a living
by working as a private consultant

he now resides alone
in a two-bedroom flat
close to chelsea beach

he attends
spoken-word poetry readings in the city
on saturdays
almost religiously

sometimes he wins prizes
in spoken or written
poetry competitions
and feels affirmation
that his life is perhaps –
finally –
on the right path

memory

the experience of living alone
was new
and it was extraordinary

whenever I had to leave my little flat
to go to work
it was with trepidation

the world *out there*
felt like a scary place

> *when I finished*
> *my work commitments*
> *I could feel myself almost running*
> *to return to the four walls*
> *that had come to comprise*
> *my home*
> *and my idea*
> *of freedom*

I stuck printouts
of some of my poems
to the walls of the flat

my own equivalent
of hung art

a declaration
of my personhood

2006

past

pluto
is demoted

it is no longer considered
a planet

saddam hussein
is hanged
for crimes against
humanity

the first australian casualty
of the invasion of iraq
shoots himself
while skylarking with a gun

a practicing poet is
the nursing unit manager
of a regional psychiatric service

he marries
a singer and songwriter

a puppeteer

413 mm of rain falls
in beechworth

history

frank has re-trained
as a clinical psychiatric nurse
in order to earn
a more regular income

he is continuing to develop his skills
as a poet
and is about to self-publish
a second collection of poems

he and his new partner
will set up house together
in regional victoria
along with their border collie

memory

I was required to invest thirty days
in unpaid shifts
to renew my clinical nursing skills
and re-qualify
as a psychiatric nurse

it was
an extraordinary experience
and resulted in much
good poetry

there were so many
stories
that needed to be told

as soon as I had earned the renewal
of my practicing certificate
I was snaffled to nurse-manage
a rural psychiatric facility

they were having
a few problems

and . . .

I was in
a new relationship

setting up house

as difficult as the work could be
these were wonderful
and exciting experiences

2011

past

there is a hot white dwarf
in ursa minor

amy winehouse dies
of alcohol poisoning

in australia the bones
of ned kelly
the nineteenth-century bushranger
are located
in an unmarked grave

a poet
and his wife
and their dog
are now residents of the township
of stanley

about ten kilometres
above beechworth

he has begun to measure
the rainfall on their property

1240 mm of rain falls
in beechworth

history

the family unit
lives on a two-acre property
up in the hills

frank works
as a rostered psychiatric nurse
in the local acute psychiatry service

his professional career has travelled
in a full circle
from its beginnings

up and down
the slippery slope

with his wife's assistance
he has now self-published
three books of poetry
and feels entitled
to consider himself an author

350mm of rain falls
on the property
in the spring

memory

I eventually burnt myself out
in the management job

started working longer
and longer days
and more of them
without a break

until I couldn't cope anymore

we moved to beechworth
and then up the hill
to stanley

I transitioned to a job
'on the floor'
of an acute psychiatric ward

it was very strange
working back in beechworth
where I grew up

I would experience
full-on panic attacks
when I visited the township
because I was remembered
by so many people as *george's son*

and they expected me
to remember them
but I did not

I did not

2016

past

there are no more
videocassette recorders
being produced

'pokemon go'
introduces augmented reality
to mobile phones

in australia
the census
is intended to be taken
online

a cyber-attack denies service

a poet discovers the work
of the french philosopher
gaston bachelard
and cannot stop writing
for weeks

1430 mm of rain falls
in beechworth

history

frank and his family
are resident
in beechworth again

he continues to work for pay –
as a nurse in a psychiatric hostel
and to develop his own story-telling style
of writing poetry

he is learning the bare rudiments
of playing ukulele
without great flair or mastery

1,295 mm of rain falls
in the backyard

memory

I became a part-time nurse
and
a full-time poet

being able to play a ukulele
and having some of my words
put to music
was like the fulfilment
of a dream

we had a limited
social circle
but it seemed to be
enough

the life we led was –
perhaps –
only a small one

but
it was made large
through our own creativity

2021

past

a new telescope
is launched

the *james webb*
sees everything

on earth
it is estimated
that there have been
a hundred million cases
of the covid virus

in australia
a plague of mice
strips food and other items
from supermarket shelves
in gulargambone

a nurse prepares to retire
from psychiatry

he continues
to write
and to publish poetry

1285 mm of rain falls
in beechworth

history

frank has become
increasingly disenchanted
with his work as a nurse
and with psychiatry

he believes that the work he does
has become
professionally unrecognisable
and he no longer enjoys it

he has discovered
print-on-demand book publication
and formed his own
publishing imprint

frank now has over a dozen
of his own poetry books
in worldwide distribution

1,291 mm of rain falls
in the backyard

memory

the nature of work changed

there was yet another new broom
sweeping through
and I'd had
just about enough
of that kind of thing

I didn't agree with the changes
and didn't really have the patience
to go along with them

I thought it might be time
to pull the pin on psychiatric nursing
soon

I wanted to keep working
on the design and layout
of my own books
and needed to get better
at the technical side of that

I was proud to have so much
of my own work in book formats

my new goal was to get *all*
of my work
into books
and distributed
right around the world

glorious

who'd have thought

2026

past

no information
on world events
is currently available

in australia
no information
has yet become available

no information
regarding a man –
a poet –
turning seventy
has yet become available

no rainfall data is yet available
for beechworth

history

no information
is currently available

memory

no information
is currently available

PART 4

Epilogue

I do not like (and only write)

I do not like
to think
about such things

the man-made disaster
that I am a part of

the contemplation
of all that has been done
to cause

of all that should be done
to cure

(but will not be)

of what role
I should play
to relieve my own culpability

(but will not)

I do not like
to think about such things
but . . .

I will write

pen my poems

allow a little more anger
to vent through my words
than I have been accustomed
to do

PART 5

The Glossary of Terms and Phrases

I sing (a car a train an aeroplane)

Glossary Term: acoustic ecologies

why don't you
change your frequency

you're drowning out
the world

I can't hear myself
speak

I'm not sure
what I'm saying
anymore

you're too LOUD

you're too MUCH

you're too EVERYWHERE

I learnt to speak
by listening
to my mum

she made word sounds
and cooed
so I could copy

sang songs for me

I couldn't hear her
now
wouldn't be able
to talk at all

it's making me crazy
I open my mouth
and a car engine
comes out

trams and trains
and trucks

I go to sing
and
I'm an aeroplane

if I call out
nobody hears me
nobody
understands me

it's you

it's because
of YOU

you're shouting
over the top
of everything
all of the time
and everywhere
all at once

SHUT UP

shut up
and let me speak

an old song (seeking new ears)

Glossary Term: audience

do-de-do-do

do-de-do-do

save the planet
save the creatures
getting tired
of trying to teach ya

oh hello
I'm just writing
a new song

well
it's not a new song
really

weather's changing
fires are storming
I've been preaching
from dusk to dawning

really
I'm just trying
to dress it up
in a new way
so it'll sound fresh
to listeners
who have heard it all before

and to find
someone new
to sing it to
as well

someone who'll listen
to the meaning
and not just the words
or the melody

a lot of people
have heard it all before
and don't want to be bored
by the *same-old*
same-old

others know the lyrics
better than I do

they can sing them
better than I can
too

louder and clearer

too loud
I sometimes think

> *lost a lizard*
> *a vanished orchid*
> *I used to see them*
> *when I went walking*

I'm after someone else

someone who –
maybe –
doesn't know it all
already

who'll listen
and think

then
listen again
and *do*

it feels like
I've been chasing them
forever

spring is summer
summer's too long
think we're dying
hope that I'm wrong

anyway
did you want to hear
my latest . . .

do-de-do-do

do-de-do-do

come lately's (not us)

Glossary Term: blow-in

listen to them
will you

rabbiting on
about how we –
we
mind you –
should be looking after
our own land

how we should be
farming it

growing things

> *oh*
> *look out . . .*
>
> *don't tread on that*
> *native grass*
>
> *oh*
> *look out . . .*
>
> *don't cut that tree*
> *for firewood*
>
> *look out . . .*

I could give them
look out

I've been here
for generations

my family
have farmed
and looked after this land
since forever

we know
how to manage it
very well
I reckon

we don't need to be told
what to do
or what to worry about
by a bunch of
eco-come-latelys
who think they're so
city-smart
while we're all
country-dumb
and bumpkins

they won't get a look-in
around here

we know what we know
and that'll do
thanks very much

and don't get me started
on the indigenous mob

they don't say that much
but they look at us
like we've only been here
five minutes

I can't stand *that*
either

without reason (we are punished)

Glossary Term: cause for alarm/no cause for alarm

up north
they've had repeated floods

houses washed
and wet
and left to rot

stinking

nothing salvageable

poor bastards

but
our place
is a long way
away

up in the hills

a couple of hundred miles
from where those waters
rise

so
we're okay

~

in countries
overseas
like spain
and greece

brazil
and canada

they're having fires
all the time now

all the time
and hotter

at least
that's how it seems

and
around here
we get fierce fires
too

anyplace
with forest
will be prone to burn

but last year
and the year before
there was
none of that

good years they were
where
a bit of grass
was all that went up

a few acres
of national park scrub

nothing
to raise a sweat about

not like
in twenty-twenty

thank god
they weren't like that

this year . . .

well
if we keep our fingers
crossed
we should be
alright

yes
we'll be alright
again
I think

~

this morning
I nearly fell
through the floor
when I opened up
the mail

the quote came in
to insure our house
and . . .

I don't think
that
we can pay

it's too much

too high

I'm wondering
if it's still worth it
when
where we live
has always been
safe
from those disasters

why should *we*
have to pay
when
we're not the ones
with wet feet

with property
smouldering

it doesn't seem right

feels like
we're being punished
unjustly

without reason

it's a bit
of a worry

I was calm (and then the rumours started)

Glossary Term: contagion of anxiety

it's been quick

I can remember being cool
and calm
about
pretty much anything

pretty much
everything

but then
the rumours started

> *something*
> *out of china*
>
> *something*
> *from up north*
>
> *something*
> *could be lethal*

and
even if it was
just a treatable thing

> *the treatment wasn't*
> *in the country yet*
>
> *wasn't strong enough*
> *yet*

there wasn't enough
of it

it could do you harm

leave you scarred

do brain damage
to your kids

it really wasn't
that long ago
there was none of this

even now
I can't tell you
where the rumours
came from

no one took them seriously
anyway

then
it was on the news
and they brought in
restrictions

travel

movement

being in public

masks

lock down

and these mongrels
coming into the country
from other places
and then breaking out
of quarantine . . .

suddenly I find that I am
potentially
a very violent man

I want to do *them*
harm
for putting me
and the whole damn country
at risk

I don't want to talk
to my neighbours . . .

if it comes to it
I don't even want
to step outside my door
anymore

in fact
the street outside
is deserted
so I'm guessing
the neighbours feel
the same as I do

they'll be stuck inside
and glued
to the idiot box
to find out
what happens next

I’m not afraid
to admit
that I’m scared

and I can’t help
wondering
if the damn thing
might even get in
through the cracks

maybe I should organise
some draft stoppers . . .

just in case

christ
I’m sick of this

anything is possible (in springtime)

Glossary Term: contagion of hope

it is easy . . .

so easy
to despair

it is

a feeling

an emotion

a place

too readily found

a quick look around
reveals more reasons
than enough

deliberate desolation

extinctions and wipe outs

weather changes
for the worse

temperatures rising and bushfires
raging

all over the world

war and annihilation

genocide

how did it come
to this . . .

we know the answer to that
but
what can be done

who
will do it

we are so small –
each of us –
and all these things
are all
too much

it seems impossible
to live a life
without contributing
to its demise

despair . . .

why not

why not

~

this morning
I am aware
of the season

I write
on the first day
of october

the second month
of spring

small change

in recent weeks
I have been wandering
the garden

noticing the first burst
into blossom
(too soon
there is still frost

there is still
weather happening)

noticing
the rise of a plant
that I had thought
dead
due to neglect
and unfavourable conditions
(my fault
I am a poor gardener)

today
I am almost overwhelmed
by the verdancy
of new-formed leaves
on the old oak trees
at the back of the yard

almost blinded
by green
in the early morning sun

the garden
is stirring

life
is stirring

the young bottlebrushes
will blossom this year

possibly profusely

I intend
to rejoice
in the deep and royal
purple colouring
of the artichokes
when they open

I remember
the extraordinary beauty
of small florets
on a succulent plant
that is nothing much to look at
until . . .

the feeling
as I gaze on and around
and as I touch
the leaves
and flowers
of this simple garden
is joy

it is a hope that
my awareness of the trouble
this world is in
and my own sense
of a personal helplessness
cannot diminish

this
is springtime

I believe that
anything
is possible

we wish you well (in a news-free world)

Glossary Term: contagious

NEWS FLASH

it has been reported
that a new strain
of virus WeP–1
has begun to affect
members of the public randomly
throughout a number
of metropolitan suburbs
and regional centres

initial effects appear to be
uncontrolled crying

more news
as it happens

she did not know
where the tears
came from

what had caused them

nothing bad
had happened
nothing emotional

a new report
on the television news
said that many
now
were crying

when some were told
they should just
stop

it seemed
they all wept
harder

unable
or unwilling
to control it

NEWS FLASH

local authorities
are urging people to remain
within
a half-block radius
of their homes

the fear
is that contact between
a WeP–1 affected person
and non-affected persons
from a different neighbourhood
may trigger
a transmission

there are reports
now
of people crying
uncontrollably
all over the country

just repeating –
local authorities are urging people
to stay close to home
until the transmission process is clarified
and a vaccine can be developed

more news
as it happens

he wished
he could stop
sobbing

three days
had already passed

he could not eat

he could not sleep

he could not leave
the house

as frightened as he was
of the illness
that he seemed to have
he was just as afraid
of spreading it
to someone else

he couldn't bear the thought
of that

so he sat
in the lounge room
watched the tv news
and wept

NEWS FLASH

in the latest
bizarre development
shoppers have begun to hoard
facial tissues

apparently
victims of the WeP–1 virus
can't get enough of them
to try to mop up
their own tears

family members are reported
to be purchasing
huge quantities
of tissues
and placing them
on front porches
to avoid contact
with the sufferers

in related news
the death toll
of sufferers of the virus
has begun to climb

in most cases
the cause of death
is said to be exhaustion
combined with malnutrition . . .

. . . excuse me
I . . .
this is just so sad I . . .

VOICEOVER

we'll be back
with more news
on the hour

it seemed
as though —
sometimes —
normal weeping occurred

unrelated
to the virus

when it was announced
on the news
for instance
that someone had been unable
to stop crying
until they'd died

then viewers themselves
might shed a tear
sympathetically
but
only for a moment

it was important
to show control . . .

that you could stop

that it was only
because of the bad news
and not a symptom
that you had caught
the virus

the tv news
was full of stories
about people
spreading the disease

it seemed like
the whole world
was crying
and couldn't stop

NEWS FLASH

in the latest development
the government has declared
a state of emergency

lockdown and curfew
are now
in effect

emergency supplies
of rations
will be delivered to driveways
and can be collected by residents
between the hours of . . .

despite the terrible and tragic
death toll caused by the virus . . .

(see our online deaths tracker here . . .)

reports
have begun to filter in
of spontaneous recoveries
including one person
who stopped weeping
when at the point of death

we'll bring you more news
when our reporter
can get closer

she reached the point
where she couldn't stand it
any longer

she knew
that she was crying herself
to death

that everyone
was crying themselves
to death

in her despair
she turned off the news

did not want
to hear . . .

to *see*
anymore

surprisingly
her weep
became
a sob

a hiccough of a thing

her eyes
were still moist

still leaking
but . . .

NEWS FLASH UPDATE

a network reporter
has been badly injured
while trying to approach a survivor
for an interview

reports indicate
this news service itself
was being blamed
for causing the spread
of the WeP–1 virus
by broadcasting the news of it

this network categorically denies
any involvement
in the broadcasting
of a virus

we'll bring you more news
on the hour

there seemed to be
word of mouth reports
of a new wave
of tears
spreading from house to house
where people
had died

not virus-related though

this was apparently
people crying normally
over loved ones
who had died

people
who had themselves recovered
after they turned off
the news

too late
to save their family
husbands
wives
parents
friends

their children

tears of sadness
and
of rage

NEWS FLASH

reports of spontaneous recovery
from the virus
continue to come in
on a hearsay basis

increasingly
it seems no one
in the community
is prepared to speak
with our broadcast service
which is increasingly
carrying popular blame
for spread of the virus

we'll bring you more news
when it is
to hand

from neighbourhood
to neighbourhood
the word was being passed

in place of the news
silent vigils
were being held

survivors –
emaciated
and sickly in appearance –
dry-eyed and sad

dry-eyed
and angry

were gathering
to comfort
one another

occasional tears
were met with hugs

with human contact

without fear

the contagion
of WeP–1
was over
and the news
was switched
off

NEWS FLASH

this will be the last network news
broadcast

in a bizarre coincidence
as the general recovery
from effects of the virus
has continued
viewers and listeners
have been increasingly switching off
their televisions
and broadcast services

as a result
we have only a small remnant
audience
which is not commercially viable

we wish you well
iand thank you
for tuning in

there will be no
further
updates

here we are (get out of the way)

Glossary Term: convicts; in place

we stole horses
once
we *australians*

we picked pockets
and held up travellers
on the highways

manslaughter
rape and other violence
could all bring us here
from old england
so far away

and when we got here
we did
what we knew to do

here
the same
as *there*

robbery and theft

murder
manslaughter
and rape

the strong survived
the brutality
somehow
and passed it on
down the line

strength
you know
is measured
in relativities

~

today
we cry . . .

society cries

it weeps for a kinder
a *gentler*
australia

> *by now*
> *we*
> *should have changed*
>
> *these are times*
> *of inclusion*
>
> *of correction*
>
> *of apology*

do we not . . .

can we not
aspire now to more
and to better

would that not be
a little more
australian

~

small change

we were convicts
once

sent from *there*
to *here*
for our sins

for big ones
and small

we were punished
that way

we were taught

and we learned
to commit the same crimes

to do
all
the same things

might is power and power
is the law

we do
what we have always done

we do it with the law
on our side

more for the powerful

less
for the oppressed

what has changed . . .

nothing

what is different . . .

nothing

we are here
and here we stay
look to yourself and . . .

keep out
of the way

feels like (I am weeping)

Glossary Term: discomfort

I feel uneasy

I think I can . . .

I think
I *am*

I think I could . . .

I *think*
I should

but I think
it is not
enough

and I think
I should be doing
more

I believe
everything
is doomed to fail
no matter what *I* do

I wonder
if I should
forget about it all

yes
I *should*
just
forget about it all

I *will*
forget about it all

~

in the nighttime
I wake up

I don't know
why
but here I am
eyes open

wide awake

not sleeping

I have a feeling
like
I should have done . . .

something

like I *could* have done
something

like
it is too late now
my moment is gone

like
I *ought* to weep

yes

yes
I feel just like
I ought to *weep*

and *look* . . .

and *feel* . . .

these
are tears
to wet my face
and I . . .

I *feel*
like I am weeping

sometimes yes (is all it needs)

Glossary Term: empowering

sometimes
all it takes
is a little word

yes

sometimes
it is hard to know
where
that will lead

but the chance
is there

take it up
or leave it

sometimes
a yes
is all it takes

and
is all
you need

a door left ajar (roll up)

Glossary Term: endling

roll up roll up
see the last
of its kind

roll up
here
for a short time
only

roll up
the show will end
soon

roll up roll up
come see
before its gone

roll up

~

inside the tent
a front row
chair

a cage of bars
a creature
pacing

up and back

then

up and back

again

restless restless
anxious looks

eyes everywhere

a *yip*

a *howl*

a creature
pacing

~

roll up roll up
come see the show

roll up
this one time
only

roll up roll up
there's only today left

roll up now
all gone
tomorrow

~

inside the tent
there is room
to spare

the show
is a cage
that is empty

a door
that can now
be left ajar

at the end (is home)

Glossary Term: erratic landscape

where is this . . .

why am I . . .

how . . .

above to below

roll

from above
to below
roll

here I am

because I am

one turn comes after
another

from above
to below

roll

here I am

here
I remain

at the end
of the roll
is me

above
below

all that
is one

the end of the roll
is home

at the end
of my roll
is home

reminiscence (with an old god)

Glossary Term: geological time

do you remember the day
when the moon
was born

so many long cycles
ago

do you remember the time
when the plants
turned green

under the sun
aeons ago

and do you recall the season
when the ice caps
formed

yes
that was so cold
ages ago

and the movement of tides
when creatures first swam

and crawled

and then walked

that too was a time
many thousands
of years ago

~

I still recall
when I first saw you

yes
I saw *you* . . .

it seems like
it was just
a moment
ago

maybe (a biscuit)

Glossary Term: glacial milk

well first
you need to grind
your rock . . .

glacial grind
I mean

over a long
long time

you'll end up
with a lovely slurry
of what used to be
bedrock

that's your basic
glacial flour

now
you mix that in
with water
to get yourself
a cup . . .

well no
not a cup

more like
a *river*
of glacial milk

what can you do
with it . . .

well
I suppose
if you slushed it all up
together with
some other ingredients

chocloate
sugar
butter

whatever

I suppose *then*
you could maybe
pour the mixture on a tray
and pop it into a volcano
to cook

a glacier biscuit
for a norwegian troll . . .

maybe

seeing (is real-ing)

Glossary Term: ground truthing

I saw it
in the pictures

images
taken by a satellite

or
by someone on the ground there
hardwiring a jpeg through
to their editor

to get the pic
onto the newsfeeds
and all the online
publications

it looked horrific

such shocking images

of the war in . . .

of the flood that swept away . . .

of the fires that raging across . . .

of entire suburbs locked down

of the open graves
that occupied acres of land
waiting for the bodies
to fill them

but
it's all a bit *unreal*
isn't it

I mean
I know
that all these things
are happening

I *know* because I can see
that it is so
but . . .

there's a disconnect

I *know*
but I do not
feel

until they happen
here

to me
and to mine

until I hear the names
called
that are places
that I know

names named
who are people
that I have met

touched

spoken to

until I kick
the ash
after the fire
has passed

no
until I see the flames
approaching
where I am

until . . .

it just isn't . . .

it doesn't feel
real

I have to see

go ahead (one hop at a time)

Glossary Term: hasten slowly

> *what*
> *is* progress
>
> *how far*
> *is* far
>
> *how much of a thing*
> *is enough*

it doesn't have to happen
all at once

it's ok
to take it slowly

conquering the universe
needs time

and little steps

look around

not everything is fast
but
some things
keep on moving

maintaining
momentum

creeping forward
all the time

like . . .

a cane toad crossing australia

sometimes hopping

sometimes sitting

sometimes hitching a ride
on a truck

and sometimes
breeding up
for the next step forward

sometimes . . .

suddenly
there they are
in western australia
somehow

it doesn't have to be
all at once

take your time

make your plans

then go ahead
one hop
at a time

to whom I belong (to what I am)

Glossary Term: imaginaries

I think . . .

well
I *feel*
that I am
a greenie

> *a conservationist or environmentalist,*
> *especially one who participates*
> *in protest demonstrations*

~

sometimes I have moments
as if I was a kind
of eco-warrior

> *a person who zealously pursues*
> *environmentalist aims*

~

there is a part
of me . . .

a large part of me
that I *know* to be
conservative

> *disposed to preserve existing conditions,*
> *institutions, etc., or*

to restore traditional ones,
and to limit change

~

and I am –
as well –
I am *absolutely*
a liberal

pertaining to, based on, or advocating liberalism,
especially the freedom of the individual
and governmental guarantees
of individual rights and liberties

~

I *wish*
that I knew a greater
clarity

clearness or lucidity as to perception
or understanding;
freedom from indistinctness or ambiguity

~

in the dreams I dream
I am
strong

of great moral power,
firmness, or courage

~

but mostly . . .

I am *too often*
mostly
too much
confused

> *not thinking coherently or rationally*
> *incorrectly differentiated, identified,*
> *or associated without order;*
> *jumbled disconcerted, perturbed, or ashamed*
> *expressed in a way that is not easily understood*

~

and
I believe
I have misled myself

I believe
I am completely
lost

> *gone astray or missed the way;*
> *bewildered as to place, direction,*
> *etc.*

~

I wish

oh
how I *wish* that I was
a radical

extreme,
especially as regards change
from accepted or traditional forms

~

but at heart I know
I am mostly
a pessimist

a person who habitually sees
or anticipates
the worst
or is disposed to be gloomy

~

and the place
that I belong is down
with the hopeless

providing no hope;
beyond optimism or hope;

desperate

~

yes
home for me
is among
the pessimists

the abject

and the lost
who sometimes
raise their heads
above . . .

for moments of clarity

long enough
to become confused
again

and then fall down

> *lose one's balance and collapse;*
> *collapse to the ground;*
> *be shown to be inadequate or unsuccessful; fail*

and then
I fall
back down

it sounded like (disappearing)

Glossary Term: inaudible voice

I *thought* I heard
my name
called

looked around

there was no one there

just a lonely luff
of cotton
disappearing
in a clear blue sky

and I thought
I *heard* the sound
of my name spoken aloud

looked around

the yellow tail
of a cockatoo
was cracking food open
in a she-oak tree

not paying attention to me
at all

I *know*
the sound of my name
when it is called

but
I looked around
to nothing but the breeze

ruffling a stand
of rusty black-cyprus
pines
and *my* hair as well
as it passed me by

still
it *sounded* like
my name

and I had to look around

but
there was just a glimpse
of a fat-tailed lizard

its tongue flicking blue
then
disappearing
through the undergrowth

all of them
disappearing
now

speaking to me
as they journey on

and if I listen –
quiet
and close –

I am sure
I will hear the sound
of my name called

what else (but trying)

Glossary Term: it's still worth trying

well
I don't know . . .

it seems too late

the ice
is in the water
and they say
that when it starts melting
like that
it can't be stopped

there's no turning back

and the rain . . .

well
I suppose it still rains
the way it's meant to
sometimes

somewhere

but
all of the world
seems
on fire

it will get to a point
where there is nothing left
to burn

summers
are too hot now

winters
too cold

I know
it's meant to be
that way
more-or-less
but
there's no end

there are no
limits

not anymore

storms roll in
in waves
each one stronger
than before

and I wonder
if the weather
has turned its good face
against us

and I wonder
as well
what's the point
of even trying
to stand
when it seems its so late
we're all
just falling over

but
maybe . . .

yes
maybe . . .

I can do
some thing

some
very small thing

and then one more
and
another

it may be
my day —
filled with small things —
could make
a little difference

I don't know

most likely
it's too late
but
what else am I —
are *we* —
to do

but try

a song in that (somewhere)

Glossary Term: keynote sound

well
it's true you know

hearing the wrong sounds
or too much
of them
can kill you

what do I mean . . .

well
we live
in a sort of soundscape
don't we

see
a landscape
is made up of hills
and bush
or buildings
or whatever

it's what you know
and what's natural
to you

and it's the same
with sound

you and me
are surrounded by sounds
all the time

they make up
the world that we live in
and if you hear something
that doesn't belong . . .

well
you know it in a flash
don't you
you can pick out the odd one
straight away

it's the same
for animals
and birds

they have to live in
and navigate sound
in their environment

a funny thing
about birds
is that they have to *learn*
how to sing

I mean
they're born knowing
how to sing
but they have to learn
their own songs

a robin
has to learn
a robin song

the kookaburra
has to laugh
like a kookaburra

for a lot of them
the male bird sings
and the female responds
but
she only likes
the proper song
sung by the best singer

trouble is
the world –
their world
as well as ours –
is getting noisier

so noisy they can't hear
each other too well

some of the poor young buggers
start to sing crooked
or even pick up
the songs of another species

how often have you heard
of a bird that can imitate
a telephone or a siren . . .

it's clever
but it won't likely win them
a mate

some of these birds
are dwindling
in their numbers
too

so there's even less
of them around
to do the teaching

they'll die off
in due course
all because the sounds
that they grow up with
aren't the sounds
they need to learn

there's probably a song
in that
somewhere

better (in time)

Glossary Term: lament

the sun
does not weep
when it rises
in the morning

the moon
sheds no tear
but hides her face
from time
to time

they have no choice –
those all-seeing eyes –
but to watch

all things
passing

good things
passing

I
am not strong
like the sun
to hold back tears

more like the moon
I turn away
sometimes

hide my face

sometimes
in sadness

sometimes
in shame

I am blessed –
I know –
for I do not need
to see all things

in my way
born lucky

and I know . . .

I *do* know
there will be more
when I am gone

still . . .

still
I can wish
that *now*
was a little better

perhaps –
in time –
it may be
a little better

the memories of the earth (and me)

Glossary Term: the land will hold memories

sentience

awareness
of self

the knowledge that death
will come

ability to reason
and recall

awareness
of feelings and emotions

being human –
a person –
is a multi-layered thing

it is a gift
with many edges
to ensure there is a fair chance
of incurring cuts
and other wounds
because of it

so what

it is tempting to think
that sentience
makes humans
unique

at least
to *feel* as if that is so

and each of us –
each human –
is *the most*
unique

the only *truly* unique one
in the crowd

nothing before

nothing after

until death

nothing after

does the world stop
when a human dies . . .

no
only the dead one
stops

~

I am aware
of earth –
the earth –
beneath my feet
when I am walking

try as I might
though

I can't quite believe
that the earth
is aware of *me*
in the same way

the earth

core

mantle

crust

gaia-sphere

what *consciousness* is it
that can support
such complexity

what *awareness*
that can monitor it all

react

reset

what a span of layers
and levels for
right now
to filter through

does it know
when it has been
hurt

does it know
by whom

how will it react

will it know
when I
have died

when I am gone
from my own
awareness

no
the earth will remember
other things

the way that life
grows

the colour blue

the colour green

the seasons
of the sun

I don't think
the earth
will remember
me
at all

succession planning (amid daily extinction)

Glossary Term: life persists

right now
we exist –
people exist –
by killing things

I know I know
there are some
who won't tread
on an ant

and there are some
who won't eat anything
sourced from a once-living
creature

I *know*

what I mean
is that every day
some critter or plant
or whatever
disappears off the face
of the globe we live on

and I mean
that it happens
because of what people –
humans –
do

it's a bit of a hard truth
isn't it

people are
a sort of force
of nature . . .

a force of
un-nature or *de*-nature
maybe

> *a persistent disturbance*
> *to the natural order*
>
> *an agent*
> *of constant change*
>
> *a blunt-force*
> *trauma*

it's kill kill kill

but . . .

not everything

the wilderness
that is the earth
keeps changing too

we let a housecat
run loose
and suddenly
there's a new apex predator
in the game

let a bunny run free
and we're tripping over rabbit holes
in the paddocks
and the bush

bad luck bilby
bad luck quoll

hello cane toad
hello fox

hello feral deer

it's all
a state of change

killing something off . . .

replacing it
with something else

life goes on you see
even in the great field
of killing and death-dealing
that we inhabit

it'll be our turn
one of these days . . .

humans
I mean

we'll come to a point
where we kill ourselves off
either by mayhem
or starvation
or whatever

the only question left
at that point will be

what life form
will succeed us

unpredictable (but records will fall)

Glossary Term: long term climate/short term weather

it rained today

it will be warm
tomorrow

this weather
is crazy

at least
I think so

light the fire
it's cold

in almost summer

then
shorts
sandals
tee shirt and sunnies
for tomorrow

every day needs predicting
by checking out
the sky
first thing
in the morning

~

it seems like
every year
now
is breaking records

the hottest day

the hottest year

the most vicious storms

the most ice
ever lost

more earthquakes and
more volcanoes

wildfires and floods

I'd better get used to it
I suppose

it is the usual
unusual
and forevermore

the only thing
I can be sure of . . .

another record
is going to fall

imagine playing the game (in reverse)

Glossary Term: magic gates

I used to play
video games

back . . .

way back
before *super mario*
and *pokémon go*

little cursor-driven
non-animations
and basic multi-level
arrangements

to play
you had to achieve
certain levels –
a number of points
perhaps –
before you could
ascend
to another level

then
you'd do it all over
again
to break through
to yet another
new level

each new level
would be harder

more complicated

you had to play
harder
and quicker
to keep achieving
the goals

if you managed
to break through
and achieve
all the levels

all
of the *magic gateways*

you became
the winner

the high scorer

whatever

imagine
playing in reverse

where every time
you break through
a magic gate
you become the loser

and the game
still gets harder

and
you have to keep playing
even if you want
to stop

when you get through –
finally –
to complete
the last level

the game
is over
and you lose

and *everyone*
loses

the game is called
climate change

we're climbing towards
the last levels
now

two year olds (in their billions)

Glossary Term: 'more than' human

I wonder if
what we try to do –
humans
I mean –
is to make a pet
of the world . . .

a pet
or a slave
perhaps

I mean
the world is a lot *more*
than just humans

a lot more
than just *me*

but
we each seem to look at it
as though every *thing*
is either
of use to me
and warranting
some special attention

or *useless*
and just there to be done with
as we see fit . . .

as an amusement

if we can
enslave it
then it has to be useful
and we can get some benefit
out of it

if we can make it a pet
it will be dependent on us
and do things we want it to
because of love

something like that
anyway

it's not enough –
for humans –
to let a thing be

or
to allow it
to just be useful
to something else
that isn't human

it's all about
us

all about
me

it's a hell of a thing
to reduce
an entire world
to primal
personal principles

like a two-year-old
really

seven
or eight *billion*
two-year-olds

one man everything (except harmony)

Glossary Term: 'more than' solo artists/individuals

I can play
harmonica

attach it
to a wire
then hang it
around my neck

just where I can reach it
with a quick breath
at the right part
of the song

and
I can sing

of *course*
I can *sing*

I've rigged up
a bass drum
so it sits
comfortably
on my back

between my shoulders

when I stamp
my foot
with a certain kind
of stamping
the bass drum
will boom away

while I strum
on my banjo-lele
to keep the tune

but
that's not all

I have an old-fashioned
car horn –
a hooter –
fixed under my arm

when I squeeze
it honks

and
a pair of brass cymbals
are strapped around my knees

it's only me
but I can make
a *big* noise

a *big* sound

the flower
on my hat
squirts a jet
of water

my bow-tie
twirls around

it makes the children laugh
but
I wonder . . .

would I be better

would people hear me
more clearly

would my songs
seem catchier

maybe sweeter

should I try to find
another voice

another
multi-instrumentalist

someone
to sing harmony
together
with me

would that let me be
more
than I am

it can be hard
to do it all

alone

I made it all (complete)

Glossary Term: novel ecosystems

I made all this

worked hard
to strike
just the right balance

paths
to walk on

curated forest
for wilderness
on one side
with
a patch of manicured lawn
on the other

it creates
a nice bit of symmetry
I think

there's a little hill
that I had built
with a sort of hut –
a hide –
on top
so I can look down
on the habitat
of smaller shrubs
and a pondage

watch the birds
as they visit

it's nice to be able
to take a break
and be a part of nature
at the same time

it's lovely
although
there's a tendency
to spiders
and insects

a wariness
of snakes

I know
they're part of it too
but
I don't want them

they aren't safe

frogs and birds
and bees in the flowers . . .

those are acceptable

they make it like
living in wild bush
that happens
to have been planned

shaped

there's no room
for the dangerous things
though

come on
let's walk the acreage
or
would you rather
use the buggy . . .

either way
is fine

I feel so good
knowing
that I made this

out here
is the only place
I can feel . . .

natural

complete

to beat tomorrow (once again)

Glossary Term: optimism

on the days
when the clouds
come in low

and the fog
falls so hard
that I am blind

I can look
into the future
like staring
into fairy-floss
only
it is not pink
but grey

if I try to touch . . .

it shies away

slips past my hand
to left

to right

there is no help
to come
from atmospheric braille

~

in the forest

just
half a mile
from home

I can keep
my eyes closed

use my nose
my other senses
to stay centred
on the path

smell the trees . . .

know they are green

feel the orchid flowers
nodding
in the breeze

hear the dew form
where the orb-weaver
lays out her plans

hold my tongue out
touch the air
and know
what tomorrow will bring

there will be
another day

there will be
another reason
to open my eyes

there will be
a purpose
for my heart

a purpose
for my heart to beat
tomorrow

once again

like friends (for hours sometimes)

Glossary Term: play favourites

well
it's not an easy question
to answer

there's sometimes
a bit of a war
going on
in my little patch
of the universe

in my backyard
I mean

me versus the white cockatoos
for instance

I love the birds –
great big idiot characters –
that are beautiful right up until
they open their mouths

but
they're a rotten
ratbag menace
as well

wreckers
and marauders
and
I can't love that

not in the garden

others though . . .

blue-bum bees
are a delight
and I try to make
places for them
to burrow
and to nest

I'm not very good at it
but I love them enough
to keep trying

same
with the blue-tongue lizards
that I see
once or twice a year
in the hotter months

I try to leave
materials
out as shelter for them
to rest in during the heat
and to stay cosy
through winter
while they hibernate

a bit of old drainpipe

a sheet of tin

a small heap of rubble

magpies
of course

we get generations of them
squawking
through the backyard
as they learn to forage

then singing

up on the roof

on a power pole

somewhere high

sometimes I think
the very best thing
I can do for them
is simply not
feed them
but make sure the ground
remains good pickings

you know
one of the creatures
that delights me
is the legless lizard

I find *them*
sometimes
by accident
when I'm working

little wrigglers
that give you a start
when you first see them

like baby snakes
only not

bloody marvellous

occasionally
I'll turn up a banjo frog
while I'm working

I call them
pobblebonks

I don't usually
do too much that's special
for any of them
but . . .

you know
they feel like they're personal

as though friends
and –
if I can –
I'll look after them

just with little things
to make sure
they're okay . . .

living
their best lives
in my backyard

I can watch
and listen to them
for hours
sometimes

hopeful (not really)

Glossary Term: projecting hope

at the twycross zoo
they call it
hope

and I suppose
that it *is* hope
of a sort

but it looks
to *me*
more like
a hologram

a cgi

a *hollow*-gram

an augmented reality
gamers symbol

an image of something
that is the opposite
of hopeful

a couple of creatures
living on the edge
and waiting
to die

I suppose the chance
to see them
as though
they are alive

in front of the viewer
raises a possibility

that there *might*
still be hope
for them

but
I'm watching
the united nations
issuing yet another
of their warnings
that nobody will listen to

they say
we're going to cook

one and a half
degrees
is looking more like
three

or four

maybe
we need a hologram
of what the weather is like
today

the day before
disaster

the day
in the middle
of disaster

the day
after the last day
when we might
have done something

but I . . .

I

am not
really
all that hopeful

nobody cares (it's gone)

Glossary Term: rage/love

it's the impotence
that causes it

cast your mind back
and look around
your childhood

what's it filled with . . .

kookaburras and magpies

wattlebirds and wrens

the sound of them
was the background
of your life
back then

your walk
to play in the local bush
was a short one

it was
near to home
and filled with the scent
of eucalyptus after rain

the golden yellow
of everlasting daisies
and the wild growing brush
that you
never even noticed

the boulders and rocks
that lined your path

the back
of that wallaby
that always saw you
first

it's the easiest thing
to love
what you grew up with . . .

the things that made you
you

and surrounded you
every day
until you
became a part
of it

that's the way
it was always
going to stay

wasn't it . . .

look around
now
at those same places

there's no short walk
to the bush

a lot of the old boulders
are gone

they've been moved

to make way
for engineered houses

built where there was never
any possibility
that the ground
would be suitable

and everything else . . .

pushed away

pushed further

pushed smaller

out of sight

out of sound

out of me

I look around
now
and I don't know this place

I don't belong
here

I wonder now
how I ever did

how can anyone belong
in places that were always
meant to be
a part
of a child's growing up

and a part of their life

forever
that are now just paving
and brick
and lawn
and poorly tended shrubbery

who cares

who cares about
what comes *next*

nobody cares
about what's gone before

nobody cares
about
what
is gone

reaching for the holy (in four touches)

Glossary Term: re-enchantment

she has gone
into the hills
to learn the art
of skinning an animal

of touching the flesh
of the creature
before it is placed
above the fire

before it reaches
the plate

gut it

skin it

tan the hide

soften it

stitch the purse

to know
what it is

what it feels like

~

he stands
within the cathedral
of a century old
sequoia grove

around fifty or so
trees
that reach the sky

he has closed his eyes
then breathed deeply
to take in what his senses
can tell him
of this place

held out his arms
to try to touch
the air

he listens
to the sound of the wind
speaking
high up
in the ancient redwoods

stumbles forward
until his hands are held
by the soft bark
of an old giant

the tree itself
is unyielding

unnoticing
of his presence

the smell of moist earth
rises
to anoint him

~

a man sits
at the bedside

his mother
has lain in the bed
for days now

attended periodically
by nursing staff
but with her consciousness
withdrawn

if her eyes have –
at times –
flown open
they appeared filled
with the dread
of dementia

right now
she is peaceful

each deep breath
followed
by another

the man
is a man
and not a man
at the same time

he is a son
here
now
watching over
his mother's final hours

holding her hand
physically
revisiting her life
mentally

and incidentally reflecting
on the fleeting nature
of his own time

the numbering
of days

there is a point
during the passage of days –
his
and hers –
when the lace curtain
at the window
rises
with the breath
of a breeze

and a gasp
of air
is followed
by a profound silence

a moment that passes
before the man realises
what has just occurred

by the time
he has summoned
those who must be summoned
his mother has gone

the face
has assumed a pallor
and a waxiness
that had not been there
mere moments before

there is no trace
of *her*
that he can find
in the body on the bed

he is stunned

left feeling
a sense of profound awe
at being witness
to the passing

~

a small herd of sambar deer
is grazing
among the sequoias
and nearby spread
of blackberries

they seem
content

serene
within their feral skins

the sunshine
paints them in dappled light

a tranquility that is
almost
spiritual

we belong (this town and me)

Glossary Term: sense of place

it's not just
a place

it is . . .

a relationship

~

when I was
a lad
it was all
that I knew

the streets
were my streets
to play on

it was
where I belonged

~

when I was
an adolescent . . .

so hard to think of
now . . .

the streets were mine
to stalk
in the night
all dressed up in my anger
and resentment

knowing there were eyes
peeping
from behind every window

it would not
let me go

I was trapped in its clutches

pinned down
and observed
like a specimen
in a jar

~

when I went away –
in an escape attempt
to the city –
I would visit sometimes

we knew each other
the streets and I

almost respectfully
because
they were still there
and I had been away
and come back

~

when I returned
to live in the town –
a little bruised
by then –
their familiarity
was a solace

something of familiar substance
beneath my feet
and
a ready acceptance
of my returned presence

~

we know each other
this town
and I

I won't claim
that I love it
for
it is a small place
with the usual
small-town limitations

but
I think I will die here
and knowing that
feels . . .

right

.
.
.

we belong

who knew (it was activism)

Glossary Term: socially engaged practice

ah crikey
I'm no activist

I don't have much time
for that stuff
really

marching
and slogan-ing

protesting and barricading

I've always thought that
was a young person's sport

I stay aware of what's happening

read a lot of news

worry a bit

that's it
though

as far as I go
generally
yet . . .

here I am
writing poetry
about the state
of play

that other people
might read

about what kind of disaster
this one is

or whatt*hat* one
might turn out to be

like the invasion
of weeds and pests

or the indifference
to ruin
of one sort
or another

and–
now I think about it–
I've written about
some of our modern wars
and quite a few
of our recent catastrophes

what does that
make me
I wonder . . .

and
I wonder
now
if activism has to be
about marching
and waving placards
and making a spectacle
of yourself
in parliament

throwing shit over
works of art
just to make a point

it could be
that writing a poem
filled up with what you see
or hear
or think . . .

it could be that
even a poem
qualifies

I suppose–
when I look at it
from *that* angle –
I might just be a bit
of a social activist
after all

who knew

pitch your voice (I will sing)

Glossary Term: sound signal

when I speak
to you
I
am singing

it is my intention . . .

my *hope*
that I will be heard

so I modulate my voice
into
ups and downs
and
louds and softs

vibrato
sometimes

when *I* speak
to *you*

I hope
you will hear me

I vibrate
from mouth
to ear

and I listen

will *you*
speak to *me*

tell me
you have heard

pitch your voice
for me alone to hear
what you are saying

a whisper
from you to me

to you
to me

pitch your voice
for me alone

I will sing
for you

call to mind (not anymore)

Glossary Term: solastalgia

in christchurch
new zealand
it was when they had
an earthquake

in australia it was –
maybe too long ago
but –
it was when port arthur
was a massacre

the place
is rebuilt

or
the place
is still there
but . . .

what *is* it
now

it is *not*
what it was

and I wish . . .

don't *you* wish
that it wasn't changed
that way

and I wish . . .

don't you wish
that *we*
were never changed
that way

because nothing
is the same
anymore

I am not
who I was

the world
has come crowding in
and
I am a stranger now
right here
where I stand

watching workmen shifting
a bunch of boulders
away
from where
they always stood

I think
they'll build some houses

make a new
little suburb

and I don't care

no
really
I don't mind

people
have to live
somewhere

they need a roof
and a boundary fence
but
there used to be
boulders there
and already
I can't recall them

they were
a part of me
and
now they're gone

all these little parts
of me . . .

I am here
in the place I've been
for my whole life

it's a place
right below my feet

in the air
I breathe
and . . .

it's a place
that I can't call
to mind
anymore

looking after one another (the best we can)

Glossary Term: stewardship

none of this
is my land

I just
place my footsteps down
upon it

give it a little
of my time

hold a leaf
that's green
to scent the flavour

sometimes
I'll tidy up
this or that

make sure the path
stays clear

touch it
with my hands
most
every day

it isn't my land
but
it may be
that it owns me

I sometimes
can't imagine
who I am
without allowing
to myself
that I am nothing
unless I'm here

I lose myself
in other places
and I end up
confused

and I'll lose myself
right here as well

the difference
is that
here
I *know*

we look after
one another
the best
we can

already in the ground (waiting)

Glossary Term: stranded assets

what if you had
a coalfield
full of coal
and
a power station
that burned it
to make power

but power
wasn't made that way
any more

> *it rays down*
> *from the sun*
>
> *it blows in*
> *with the wind*
>
> *it swims past*
> *in the water*

and you
have all this coal
but . . .
it costs
too much to make

> *it's dirty to use*

makes heat
forever
in the atmosphere

you're wealthy

like having followers
on social media

like winning the board game
monopoly

like a day to come
when they change the rules back
again

sitting on
a fortune

preparing for the day
to come

when you're going to be
one of the big guns
with assets
already in the ground

waiting

it's enough (for an old man)

Glossary Term: technologies

they sent armstrong
to the moon
on less tech
than a telephone has
now

got him and his mates
to the sea
of tranquillity
then
back home

I was just a kid
of about twelve years of age
watching with *my* mates
at school

we had
a black and white tv
mounted on
a rolling platform
at the front of the assembly hall

~

when a computer
landed on my desk
at work
it was still in its packaging

unassembled

we all looked at it
and didn't know
what to do

or how to do it

I was about thirty
years old
and knew my life was changing
right then

in that moment

~

a couple of years back
we bought a *new*
second-hand car

I was told it had
more than a hundred
individual motors in it

> *doors and locks*
>
> *windows*
>
> *window wipers*
>
> *washers*
>
> *air-con*
>
> *sensors*

all of them managed
by computer chips

my mechanic told me
he wasn't sure
how to look after modern cars
anymore

they are all technology
and not so much
mechanics

~

I read the news
on my telephone now

it seems important
to stay informed
but . . .

I fall out
of conversations
because my television
isn't connected
to the internet
and I don't watch
subscription channels

~

I'm old fashioned

and I'm writing down the first draft
of this poem of mine
with a pen

scratching the words
onto paper

as though technology
doesn't count for anything
in poetry

it feels like I'm shouting

aiming my voice
at the clouds
and thinking they might listen

too often
now
I feel old

too old
to learn the next new trick

the faster data travels
the slower I go

there comes a time –
and
I think it's now –
when to touch
and smell
and listen . . .

to see and hear things
as they are
is just about enough

for me –
old man that I am –
I think
it is enough

everything changed (over time)

Glossary Term: temporal scale

time
changes everything

from one minute
to the next

from the beginning
to the end

it's only a matter
of choose something
to measure . . .

today versus yesterday

hot versus cold

day and night

young me
to old me

hot now
hot a hundred years ago

the thickness of each ring
across a tree trunk

layers of soil
and sediment
deposited . . .

epoch
by epoch

how much
change
have I seen
in my life
and how much
has life
changed me . . .

enough
that I am grown old
and cannot tell you
when it happened

in the blink of an eye

the passing
of an instant

time has changed
everything

pebbles pebbles (landslides)

Glossary Term: tipping point/trigger

you know how it is . . .

you see it all the time
in movies

one little thing

a pebble rolling

a sudden noise
that echoes and vibrates
too much

just
an innocuous moment
that starts slowly
at first . . .

then
with more momentum

until suddenly
there's an avalanche happening
or
the dam bursts
and sweeps away everything
in front of it

it's unstoppable . . .

well
we're not there yet

I mean sure
the weather is changed

storms are fierce
and the cyclones are like

oh my god

and fires and droughts
and all that

it's predictable
that one of these things
will likely be the trigger
but see
people still feel able
to say

oh well
we've had these things happen
before

these times will pass
too

we'll be ok
again

we're getting plenty
of earthquakes too
I know

and floods

we're not there yet
though

I'm not wishing it
no
but I think
it's going to take something
different

maybe australia
or america

russia or china

one of these big
and wealthy countries
to start having crop failures

food shortages
to go with it

or maybe it'll take
another pandemic

an indiscriminate killer
that diminishes the ability
of exploiters and manipulators
to create profit

I don't know

I just can't help
thinking
that I can see pebbles rolling
down an unstable slope

every one of them
is a trigger

maybe *the* trigger

I was not warned (not nearly enough)

Glossary Term: trigger warning

warning:
this story contains distressing content

yes

I am sorry

I watched the news
last night
on tv

and I regret it

people drowned in spain

north koreans marched
to the frontlines
in ukraine

a child was killed
when struck by a car
while playing in the yard
at school

everybody loved him

a youth was stabbed
in an outer suburb

everybody loved him

the rainfall
in our country is changing

falling less
and
falling more

falling badly
for those of us
who thought we knew
the weather

who thought we knew
anything

.

.

.

I don't think
that I know anything
anymore

I watched the news
last night
on tv

and I wish
that they had tried
a little harder
to warn me

what they do (what I have to live with)

Glossary Term: urban/regional divide

I know
it isn't right
but
it can be easy to think
of *the city*
as being a foreign country

an alien place

from thirty miles out
the countryside
is different

it's been paved

all roads and footpaths
and houses
and subdivisions

then
it becomes freeways
and tollways

I can tell you that
for me
it's a frightening experience
to have to get on
one of their main roads
now

the press of traffic
and the myriad ways
and byways
you have to navigate
just to get off . . .

leaves me
all nerves

short of breath

you know
people even talk faster
not to mention
multiple languages
and half-english
or
slang-english

maybe the worst thing
about the city
though
isn't the physicality of it –
though that's
more than enough –
no
it's that so many of the people
that live there
think they know
what's best for *us*
who don't

back here at home
we're just as real

we've got the same issues
just as many of them

and we've got some besides –
that they never have to think about
down there
in the big smoke

they just assume
and don't take the time
to actually find out

to ask the right questions

it's politicians
mostly
but so many others
as well

everyone thinks that
it's the greenies
that are our greatest worry
but that's not right

country people
are conservationists
too

right now
if you asked me
what would be
the main concern I have . . .

it would probably be
the big companies
that buy most of our produce
for their shops

they're city-based too
and think only about
how to squeeze a few cents
off the wholesale price
of a litre of milk
or a kilo
of spuds

they make it so that
it's not worthwhile
to produce anything
or
to stay on the farm

they make it
so it's more attractive
to sell the land
than
to work it

to make more little cities
everywhere
until that
is all that this country is

I don't like
the big cities
but
I can mostly keep away
from them

what I can't dodge
is the way these city-based
decision
and policy makers
think

and the consequences
of what they do
that people like me
have to live with

where do you want (your third dimension)

Glossary Term: x/y/z coordinates

so
if you were going to draw a map
you'd want to show
north
wouldn't you

north-south

and . . .

well
it's obvious
isn't it

you want to show
east-west too

I still hanker for paper maps
from the old days
that always showed north
up at the top of the page
with everything else orientated
from that starting point

so anyway
that's your *x*
and your *y*
but
that's not enough
is it

how high
is that mountain

how deep
is the valley
or
the ocean floor

and
how can you work out
how far away
from the sun
the earth
is

that's where you need
a third dimension

that's
where you want
your *z*

PART 6

Afterwords

Index of Glossary Terms

K

L

M

N

O

P

R

S

T

U

X

Author Information

Frank Prem has been a storytelling poet since his teenage years. He has been a psychiatric nurse through all of his professional career, which now exceeds forty years.

He has been published in magazines, online zines, and anthologies in Australia, and in a number of other countries, and has both performed and recorded his work as spoken word.

He lives with his wife in the beautiful township of Beechworth in North East Victoria, Australia.

Connect with Frank

Find Frank at his website www.FrankPrem.com, or through Social Media online at Facebook, X (Twitter), Instagram and YouTube.

Other Published Works

Free Verse Poetry

Small Town Kid (2018)
Devil In The Wind (2019)
The New Asylum (2019)
Herja, Devastation - With Cage Dunn (2019)
Walk Away Silver Heart (2020)
A Kiss for the Worthy (2020)
Rescue and Redemption (2020)
Pebbles to Poems (2020)
The Garden Black (2022)
A Specialist at The Recycled Heart (2022)
Ida: Searching for The Jazz Baby (2023)
From Volyn to Kherson (2023)
Alive Is What You Feel (2023)
White Whale (2024)
Pilgrim Volume 1 - Illustrated by Leanne Murphy (2024)
A Poetry Archive Volume 1 (2024)
A Poetry Archive Volume 2 (2024)
A Poetry Archive Volume 3 (2024)
A Poetry Archive Volume 3 (2024)

Picture Poetry/Spoken Image

Voices (In The Trash) (2020)
The Beechworth Bakery Bears (2021)
Sheep On The Somme (2021)
Waiting For Frank-Bear (2021)
A Lake Sambell Walk (2021)
A Few Places Near Home (2023)
The Cielonaut (2024)

What Readers Say

Small Town Kid

A modern-day minstrel. Highly recommended.
–A. F. (Australia)

Small Town Kid is a wonderful collection.
–S. T. (Australia)

Devil In The Wind

Trust me, this book will stay with you. Bravo!
–K. K. (USA)

Moving, beautiful, and terrible. I was left with a profound sense of respect, as well as a reminder that we should never take for granted every precious every moment of life.
–J. S. (South Africa)

The New Asylum

Words can't do justice to the emotional journey I travelled in (reading this collection).
–C. D. (Australia)

If I had to pick one book over the past year that has truly resonated with me, this would be it.
–K. B. (USA)

Walk Away Silver Heart

Instantly grips you by the throat in his step-by-step story of survival. Bravo!
–K. K. (USA)

Outstanding!
–B. T. (Australia)

A Kiss For The Worthy

A Celebration of Life Written in Thoughtful Bursts of Poetic Expression
–C. M. C. (United States)

With every verse, I found myself reflecting about myself, my life, and the world.
–K.

Rescue and Redemption

The passion of love in its many forms explored by one for another.
–J. L. (United States)

I've enjoyed every word, every breath. Every moment within the life of these stories.
–C. D. (Australia)

Sheep On The Somme

Museums and archivists take note–sell this in your gift shops, preserve it in your archives. Professors, teachers–share with your students.
–A. R. C. (United States)

(This) book is a beautiful and graphic tribute to all those brave men and women who gave their lives for their countries between 1914 and 1918.
–R. C. (South Africa)

Ida: Searching for The Jazz Baby

I found myself deeply moved by the presentation of Ida's elusive, illusionary life.
–E. G. (United States)

He gives her a depth and vulnerability that the press didn't.
– A. C. (United Kingdom

The Garden Black

Prem creates verse that illuminates our world, its experiences and history.

–S. C. (United Kingdom)

Prem's poetry reminds that life is fragile and fleeting ... both harsh and beautiful.

–D. G. K. (Canada)

A Few Places Near Home

The author has captured many beautiful images in this book, and is a wonderful photographer as well as a poet. This book would make a beautiful coffee table book filled with moving prose to make us ponder with gorgeous accompanying images.

–D. K. (Canada)

www.FrankPrem.com

www.ingramcontent.com/pod-product-compliance
Lightning Source LLC
Chambersburg PA
CBHW072109110526
44590CB00018B/3373
9781923166332